Human–Computer Interaction Series

Editors-in-chief

Desney Tan
Microsoft Research, Redmond, WA, USA

Jean Vanderdonckt
Louvain School of Management, Université catholique de Louvain,
Louvain-la-Neuve, Belgium

More information about this series at http://www.springer.com/series/6033

Arun K. Kulshreshth · Joseph J. LaViola Jr.

Designing Immersive Video Games Using 3DUI Technologies

Improving the Gamer's User Experience

 Springer

Arun K. Kulshreshth
School of Computing and Informatics
University of Louisiana at Lafayette
Lafayette, LA
USA

Joseph J. LaViola Jr.
Department of Computer Science
University of Central Florida
Orlando, FL
USA

ISSN 1571-5035   ISSN 2524-4477   (electronic)
Human–Computer Interaction Series
ISBN 978-3-030-08582-7   ISBN 978-3-319-77953-9   (eBook)
https://doi.org/10.1007/978-3-319-77953-9

This Springer imprint is published by the registered company Springer International Publishing AG part of Springer Nature
The registered company address is: Gewerbestrasse 11, 6330 Cham, Switzerland

To my parents, wife, family and friends.

Preface

A 3D user interface (3DUI) is an interface that involves human–computer interaction in which the user performs tasks in three dimensions, for example, interaction using hand/body gestures, interaction using a motion controller (e.g. Nintendo Wii, Sony PlayStation Move), interaction on a virtual reality device using tracked motion controllers. All these technologies which allow a user to interact in three dimensions are called 3D user interface technologies. These 3D user interface technologies have the potential to make games more immersive and engaging and thus potentially provide a better user experience to gamers. Although 3D user interface technologies are already available for games, it is still unclear how their usage affects gameplay and if there are any user performance benefits. A systematic study of these technologies in game environments is required to understand how gameplay is affected and how we can optimize the usage in order to achieve a better gameplay experience. This book presents the current state of research in usage of 3D user interface technologies for improving the gamer's user experience. As part of this book, we have focussed on a few technologies: stereoscopic 3D, head tracking, and hand gesture-based menu systems.

Chapter 1 introduces several 3D user interface technologies which could be potentially used for games. Chapter 2 discusses stereoscopic 3D technology and its usage in games. Chapter 3 talks about usage of head tracking in games and how one could use it to design better games. Chapter 4 presents several hand gesture-based menu selection techniques. Chapter 5 discusses an experiment which explores if dynamic stereoscopic 3D parameters (convergence and separation) could enhance the depth discrimination in the scene and thus improve the overall gaming experience of the user. Chapter 6 discusses an experiment which analyses the effect of simultaneous usage of several 3DUI technologies. In Chap. 7, we discuss the implications of our experiments and propose some directions for future research. Chapter 8 summarizes the findings of our experiments and concludes this book.

Lafayette, LA, USA   Arun K. Kulshreshth
Orlando, FL, USA   Joseph J. LaViola, Jr.
February 2018

Contents

Acronyms

3D	Three dimensional
3DUI	Three-dimensional user interface
ANOVA	Analysis of variance
API	Application programming interface
CAVE	Cave automatic virtual environment
CPU	Central processing unit
CT	Computed tomography
DLP	Digital light projection
DOF	Degree of freedom
FPC	First-person controller
FPS	First-person shooter
GB	Gigabytes
GPU	Graphics processing unit
GUI	Graphical user interface
HCI	Human–computer interaction
HDMI	High-definition multimedia interface
HDTV	High-definition television
HMD	Head-mounted display
PC	Personal computer
RAM	Random access memory
S3D	Stereoscopic 3D
SDK	Software development kit
VE	Virtual environment
VR	Virtual reality

Chapter 1
3D User Interface Technologies and Games

Abstract This chapter introduces several 3D user interface technologies available for games and explains why it is important to study the affects of these technologies on the gaming experience of a user. Specifically, we have focussed on three technologies: (1) stereoscopic 3D, (2) head tracking, and (3) hand gesture based menu systems. Each of these technologies are explained along with how they can potentially improve games.

1.1 Introduction

A 3D user interface (3DUI) is an interface that involves human-computer interaction in which the user performs tasks in three dimensions. For example, interaction using hand/body gestures, interaction using a motion controller (e.g. Nintento Wii, Sony PlayStation Move), interaction on a virtual reality device using tracked motion controllers, etc. All these technologies which allows a user to interact in three dimensions are called 3D user interface technologies. In the past, 3D user interface technologies (Doug A Bowman et al. 2004) (e.g., stereoscopic 3D, head tracking, gesture based control, etc.) were mostly limited to research labs and commercial applications such as visualization (Robertson et al. 1993; Kobsa 2001; Maupu et al. 2005), 3D modeling (Liang and Green 1994; Park and Subbarao 2005) and simulation (Craighead et al. 2007). These technologies could be very useful for games. Such interfaces allow users to use natural motion and gestures to control the game thereby making the whole gaming experience more immersive and engaging. With the advancement of game interface technology, several new devices and gaming platforms (e.g., Microsoft Kinect, PlayStation Move, TrackIR 5) that support 3D spatial interaction have been implemented and made available to consumers. Currently there is plethora of games available in market which make use of these technologies.

Although 3D user interface technologies are available for games, it is still unclear how their usage affects game play and if there are any user performance benefits. For

A. K. Kulshreshth and J. J. LaViola Jr., *Designing Immersive Video Games Using 3DUI Technologies*, Human–Computer Interaction Series, https://doi.org/10.1007/978-3-319-77953-9_1

1

instance, stereoscopic 3D viewing is currently available in many games but it may not provide a better game play experience. A systematic study of these technologies in game environments is required to understand how the game play is affected and how we can optimize their usage in order to achieve a better game play experience. This book presents some of our explorations in this direction. We have specifically looked at three user interface technologies: (1) stereoscopic 3D, (2) head tracking, and (3) hand gesture based menu systems. We conducted several experiments in gaming environments to understand how the game play is affected and how can we optimize their usage in order to achieve a better game play experience. Our lessons learned from these experiments will serve as the framework for the future explorations of games which utilize 3D spatial user interface technologies.

1.2   3D User Interface (3DUI) Technologies

1.2.1   Stereoscopic 3D

Stereoscopic 3D displays present two images offset to the left and right eye of the user and these images are then fused by the brain to give the perception of 3D depth. The generation of these two images uses two stereo parameters: separation and convergence. Separation is defined as the interaxial distance between the centers of the two virtual eye camera lenses in the scene and the convergence is defined as the distance of the plane where left and right eye camera frustums intersect (see Fig. 1.1).

Stereoscopic 3D is not a new technology but it was not readily available to consumers until recently. It became popular with gamers when new 3D displays (120 Hz monitors and 3D DLP TVs) were launched which supported Nvidia 3D vision technology (released in 2008). Since 2010 many 3D TVs have been produced by TV manufacturers making it easier for consumers to get hold of 3D displays for gaming. Games are designed in 3D game engines so 3D data is already present in games. The Nvidia 3D vision driver make use of this 3D data to create stereoscopic 3D images which can be rendered on a 3D display. But the overall experience is not optimal when the games are not designed with stereoscopic 3D viewing in mind (Litwiller and LaViola 2011). Therefore, it is interesting to study how stereoscopic 3D affects game play experience and what can be done to make it better.

1.2.2   Head Tracking

Head tracking is commonly used in the virtual and augmented reality communities (Bajura et al. 1992; Marks et al. 2010; Rekimoto 1995), and has potential to be a useful approach for controlling certain gaming tasks. Recent work on head tracking

Fig. 1.1 Off-axis stereo projection

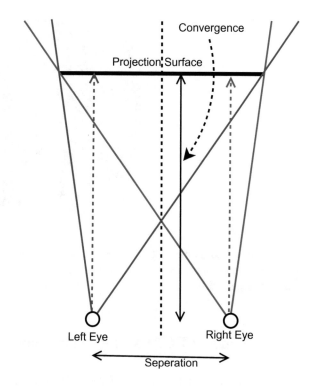

and video games has shown some potential for this type of gaming interface. In addition, previous studies (Wang et al. 2006; Yim et al. 2008) have shown that users experience a greater sense of "presence" and satisfaction when head tracking is present. It is very important to understand how head tracking affects game play experience and what kind of games make better use of head tracking. We seek to systematically explore head tracking as an interaction technique in games to be able to help game designers make better games which make optimal use of head tracking.

1.2.3   Gesture Based Menus

Menu techniques also plays an important role in video games. Since response time and ease of use of a menu system can significantly affect user experience in applications such as video games, it is essential that they be fast, efficient, and not be a burden on the user while setting up and during play. People often use fingers to count or enumerate a list of items. Menus designed based on finger count are very easy to understand and finger count gestures are fast to perform. Therefore, it is interesting to explore Finger-count menus for video games (see Fig. 1.2). These menus could

Fig. 1.2 Finger-count menu

be very useful for some in-game tasks (switching modes from first person view to third person view and vice versa in a racing game, selecting weapons in a first person shooter game, etc.).

1.3   Utilizing 3DUI Technologies for Games

We need to understand the affect of the 3DUI technologies discussed in previous section on games in order to design games which can use these technologies effectively. We will first explore these technologies in isolation to study their effects on different game genres and come up with design guidelines for their optimal usage in games. In the end, we will integrate all these technologies simultaneously in a custom designed game to understand the interplay between the technologies and their effects on the gaming experience. We conducted three experiments to examine the usefulness of stereoscopic 3D, head tracking, and finger-based menu selection in video games. Based on the lessons learned from these three experiments, we custom designed an air-combat game integrating the three 3DUI technologies (stereoscopic 3D, head tracking, and finger-count gestures) and studied the combined effect of these technologies on the gaming experience.

Firstly, we will explore the effects of stereoscopic 3d in modern motion controlled games. A previous study (Litwiller and LaViola 2011) for PC games showed that playing games in 3D stereo does not provide any significant performance benefits than with using a 2D display. However, this study used a traditional game controller (the Xbox 360 controller) as the interaction device and the games used were not designed with 3D stereo in mind. It has been shown (Bianchi-Berthouze et al. 2007; Lindley et al. 2008) that an increase in body movement imposed, or allowed, by the game controller results in an increase in player's engagement level. So for our work we focused on action controlled games using a 3D spatial interaction device. Additionally, we noticed that the existing games use fixed stereoscopic

3D parameters (convergence and separation) throughout usage time. However, this approach reduces stereoscopic depth in certain scenarios (for e.g. a game with a large depth variation between different scenes). Thus, we will also explore how can we optimize stereoscopic 3D using dynamic stereoscopic 3D parameters. We present two scenarios (see Chap. 5 for details) where optimizing the stereo parameters (separation and convergence) could enhance the depth discrimination of the user.

Secondly, we will explore the benefits of head tracking in modern video games. Head tracking has potential to be a useful approach for controlling certain gaming tasks. Previous studies (Wang et al. 2006; Yim et al. 2008) have shown that users experience a greater sense of "presence" and satisfaction when head tracking is present. However, these studies were conducted in simple game scenarios. We seek to systematically explore the effects of head tracking, in complex gaming environments typically found in commercial video games, in order to find if there are any performance benefits and how it affects the user experience.

Thirdly, we will explore the usefulness of finger-based menus. Menu systems based on finger counting are not a new technique. Finger-Count menus were first proposed for multi-touch surfaces (Bailly et al. 2010). They were later adapted for distant displays (Gilles Bailly et al. 2011), using the Kinect as the gestural input device. We will compare Finger-Count menus with other techniques in literature such as 3D Marking Menu (Ren and O'Neill 2012).

The previous three experiments has been focused on these technologies in isolation and it is unclear how the gaming experience would be affected if several 3DUI technologies are used simultaneously. By designing a game which integrates several 3DUI technologies, we will try to understand the interplay between the technologies and its effect on the gaming experience. We will discuss the design of an air-combat game integrating several 3DUI technologies (stereoscopic 3D, head tracking, and finger-count gestures) and will study the combined effect of these technologies on the gaming experience. Our game design will be based on design principles for optimizing the usage of these technologies in isolation (based on the results of the previous three experiments). Additionally, to enhance depth perception and minimize visual discomfort, the game will utilize dynamic stereoscopic 3D parameter (convergence and separation) adjustments based on the user's look direction.

1.4 Outline of the Book

In Chap. 2, we will discuss work related to benefits of stereoscopic 3D in games and the study which seeks to determine the benefits of stereoscopic 3D in motion controlled video games. This study examines if presence of motion control will enhance user performance in stereoscopic 3D environment compared to normal 2D display environment. In Chap. 3, we discuss the work related to usage of head tracking for several applications and our study which examines the benefits of head tracking in video games. In Chap. 4, we discuss the work related to menus based on finger count. Then, we discuss the study to determine the usefulness of finger-count based menu system. Finger-count menus selects an item on screen based on the number of fingers extended by the user. Chapter 5 discusses an experiment which explores if dynamic stereoscopic 3D parameters (convergence and separation) enhance the depth discrimination in the scene and thus improve the overall gaming experience of the user. Chapter 6 presents the results of a comprehensive video game study which explores how the gaming experience is effected when several 3D user interface technologies are used simultaneously. In Chap. 7, we discuss the implications of our experiments and preposes some directions for future research. Chapter 8 summarizes the findings of our experiments and concludes the book.

References

Bailly G et al. (2011) Comparing free hand menu techniques for distant displays using linear, marking and finger-count menus. In: Human- computer interaction INTERACT 2011, vol. 6947. LNCS. Springer, Berlin, pp. 248–262. ISBN: 978-3-642-23770-6. https://doi.org/10.1007/978-3-642-23771-3_19

Bailly G, Lecolinet E, Guiard Y (2010) Finger-count & radial-stroke shortcuts: 2 techniques for augmenting linear menus on multi-touch surfaces. In: Proceedings of the SIGCHI conference on human factors in computing systems. CHI'10, ACM, New York, USA, 2010, pp. 591–594. https://doi.org/10.1145/1753326.1753414

Bajura M, Fuchs H, Ohbuchi R (1992) Merging virtual objects with the real world: seeing ultrasound imagery within the patient. In: SIGGRAPH Computer Graphics 26.2 (July 1992), pp. 203–210. ISSN: 0097- 8930. https://doi.org/10.1145/142920.134061

Bianchi-Berthouze N, Kim WW, Patel D (2007) Does body movement engage you more in digital game play? and why?. In: Proceedings of the 2nd international conference on affective computing and intelligent interaction. vol. 4738, pp. 102–113

Bowman DA et al. (2004) 3D user interfaces: theory and practice. Addison-Wesley

Craighead J et al. (2007) A survey of commercial open source unmanned vehicle simulators. In: 2007 IEEE international conference on robotics and automation. Apr. 2007, pp. 852–857. https://doi.org/10.1109/ROBOT.2007.363092

Kobsa A (2001) An empirical comparison of three commercial information visualization systems. In: IEEE symposium on information visualization, 2001. INFOVIS 2001, pp. 123–130. https://doi.org/10.1109/INFVIS.2001.963289

Liang J, Green M (1994) JDCAD: a highly interactive 3D modeling system. Comput. Graph. 18(4):499–506

Lindley SE, Le Couteur J, Berthouze NL (2008) Stirring up experience through movement in game play: effects on engagement and social behaviour. In: Proceeding of the twenty-sixth annual SIGCHI conference on human factors in computing systems. New York, NY, USA: ACM, 2008, pp. 511–514

Litwiller T, LaViola Jr JJ (2011) Evaluating the Benefits of 3D Stereo in Modern Video Games. In: Proceedings of the SIGCHI Conference on Human Factors in Computing Systems. CHI'11. New York, NY, USA: ACM, 2011, pp. 2345–2354. https://doi.org/10.1145/1978942.1979286

Marks S, Windsor JA, Wunsche B (2010) Evaluation of the effectiveness of head tracking for view and avatar control in virtual environments. In: 25th international conference of image and vision computing New Zealand (IVCNZ), Nov. 2010, pp. 1–8. https://doi.org/10.1109/IVCNZ.2010.6148801

Maupu D et al. (2005) 3D stereo interactive medical visualization. In: Computer graphics and applications, IEEE 25.5, Sept. 2005, pp. 67–71. ISSN: 0272- 1716. https://doi.org/10.1109/MCG.2005.94

Park S-Y, Subbarao M (2005) A multiview 3D modeling system based on stereo vision techniques (English). In: Machine vision and applications 16.3 (2005), pp. 148–156. ISSN: 0932-8092. https://doi.org/10.1007/s00138-004-0165-2

Rekimoto J (1995) A vision-based head tracker for fish tank virtual reality-VR without head gear. In: Proceedings virtual reality annual international symposium, March 1995, pp. 94–100. https://doi.org/10.1109/VRAIS.1995.512484

Ren G, O'Neill E (2012) 3D marking menu selection with freehand gestures. In: IEEE symposium on 3D user interfaces. IEEE 2012, pp. 61–68

Robertson GG, Card SK, Mackinlay JD (1993)Information visualization using 3D interactive animation. Commun ACM 36(4), 57–71. ISSN: 0001-0782. https://doi.org/10.1145/255950.53577

Wang S et al. (2006) Face-tracking as an augmented input in video games: enhancing presence, role-playing and control. In: Proceedings of the SIGCHI conference on human factors in computing systems. CHI '06. Montral, Qubec, Canada: ACM, 2006, pp. 1097–1106. ISBN: 1-59593-372-7. https://doi.org/10.1145/1124772.1124936

Yim J, Qiu E, Nicholas Graham TC (2008) Experience in the design and development of a game based on head-tracking input. In: Proceedings of the 2008 conference on future play: research, play, share. Future Play '08. Toronto, Ontario, Canada: ACM, 2008, pp. 236–239. ISBN: 978-1-60558-218-4. https://doi.org/10.1145/1496984.1497033

Chapter 2
Stereoscopic 3D for Video Games

Abstract This chapter discusses related work on using stereoscopic 3D for several applications (including gaming tasks). Discussion on related work includes work on interaction between stereoscopic 3D and other motion cues. Our experiment which studies the effect of stereoscopic 3D on modern games is also presented. This experiment compares stereoscopic 3D with monoscopic 2D with a motion controller as the interaction device. We present the results of our experiment along with guidelines for the game designers who wish to use stereoscopic 3D for improving the gaming experience.

2.1 Introduction

Stereoscopic 3D technology has been around for decades and been found to be beneficial depending on the task involved (Arthur et al. 1993; Hubona et al. 1999; Munz et al. 2004; Teather and Stuerzlinger 2007). Much of the research to date has focused on simple, isolated tasks in virtual environments, and there has been very little research involving more complex tasks and richer graphical environments, such as games. In this chapter we explore the benefits of stereoscopic 3D in games. As the technology has started to become more available to consumers, game designers are incorporating stereoscopic 3D technology in games. However, it is unclear how 3D stereo affects gameplay and the user experience. Are there any measurable benefits when playing games using stereoscopic vision? In other words, do gamers gain a performance advantage when using a 3D stereo display and, if so, why? By understanding these performance benefits and the reasoning behind them, we hope to gain insights into ways that games can be made more enjoyable and help users to play them more effectively. In the next section we are going to discuss research related to stereoscopic 3D and then we will discuss a usability experiment exploring the benefits of stereoscopic 3D.

© Springer International Publishing AG, part of Springer Nature 2018
A. K. Kulshreshth and J. J. LaViola Jr., *Designing Immersive Video Games Using 3DUI Technologies*, Human–Computer Interaction Series,
https://doi.org/10.1007/978-3-319-77953-9_2

2.2 Related Work

2.2.1 Benefits of Stereoscopic 3D

Hubona et al. found that 3D stereo in a game is a more effective depth cue than shadows in a user's perception of 3D, based on accuracy and speed with which users completed gaming tasks (Hubona et al. 1999). Stereo has also been found to help users playing a game in which they eliminate targets by moving objects into defined zones. The game was still a simple task of moving a cursor to a target in the virtual world that contains objects that needed to be manipulated. To simplify the task only one object was present during the experiment (Fujimoto and Ishibashi 2005). Another study has concluded that binocular viewing in the real world as well as virtual worlds may benefit the user over monocular viewing, and while 3D stereo has been shown to be useful for depth ordering of objects in a virtual world, it may be impossible to measure how accurate a user's perception of 3D stereo is Treadgold et al. (2001). Menendez et al. (2001) have hypothesized that stereoscopic viewing would benefit a user in a flight simulation environment, but have yet to test the hypothesis.

Litwiller and LaViola explored benefits of 3D stereo in modern PC based games using the Nvidia 3D Vision Kit. No significant advantage was found in user performance over a 2D display (Litwiller and LaViola 2011). Another study evaluated game performance with a shooter game on autostereoscopic displays (Rajae-Joordens 2008) but found no differences in performance for stereo vs. monoscopic vision modes. The same study further revealed that the 3D display mode evoked significantly higher positive emotions and stronger feelings of presence than the 2D mode and was highly preferred by a large majority of the participants. An increased engagement and preference for stereoscopic games was also confirmed in Litwiller and LaViola (2011), Schild et al. (2012). The latter further found effects varying strongly across different games and target groups. Stereo evoked higher immersion and presence, especially in males, and affected attention in a way that indicates a more natural, less self-reflective gameplay. Depth perception tends to be underestimated by users in virtual environments (Jones et al. 2008), and for some selection tasks in 3D space, a one-eyed 2D cursor can be more beneficial than a 3D cursor (Ware and Lowther 1997).

The medical field has also studied the effects of 3D stereo. Stereoscopic 3D viewing significantly improves performance in robotic-assisted laparoscopic surgeries on bench models (Munz et al. 2004). Another study showed higher user performance in endoscopic tasks (pegboard, incision and suturing) when using the 3D display than the 2D display (Yamauchi and Shinohara 2005). Kickuth et al. (2002) compared effectiveness of standard CT scan vs stereoscopic 3D CT scan to in classification of acetabular fracture. Their analysis did not demonstrate any benefit in stereoscopic 3D CT compared with standard 3D CT.

2.2.2 Performance with Display Type

Research has been conducted on how well users perform with different types of 3D displays as well. Grossman and Balakrishnan looked at volumetric displays and concluded that for the simple tasks that were presented to users, stereo 3D always helped over simple perspective and though volumetric displays were more helpful for simple scenes, there was no benefit over normal 3D displays in more complex scenes (Grossman and Balakrishnan 2006). Fully immersive virtual environments have also been shown to be more effective than stereoscopic desktop environments for certain tasks. In comparing a real world scenario of oil well path editing, researchers found that a fully immersive environment, such as a CAVE, was more effective than a stereoscopic desktop environment (Gruchalla 2004). A similar study showed results that also suggested the immersive environment provided benefits to the user in analyzing data; however, it also concluded that users were more comfortable using the interaction techniques on the desktop environment (Arns et al. 1999). Stereo has been shown to increase the size and amount of abstract data that can be viewed and understood, and the benefits were only increased with a higher resolution stereoscopic display (Ware and Franck 1996; Ware and Mitchell 2005). Jin et al. (2007) compared autostereoscopic displays with 2D displays. They concluded that stereoscopic 3D mode has some advantages but it also has drawbacks of discomfort and a reduction of resolution, brightness and color saturation. Another study on autostereoscopic displays (Rajae-Joordens 2008) showed that 3D displays provoke significantly higher positive emotions and stronger feelings of presence than 2D displays in the gaming application, and are highly preferred by a large majority of the participants.

2.2.3 Interplay with Interaction Technique and Motion Cues

The interplay between 3D stereo and interaction technique has led to conflicting results. In one study, the interaction technique was found to be significant while stereo was not (McMahan et al. 2006). However, this finding has been somewhat contradicted by Teather and Stuerzlinger, who presented different positioning techniques that were dependent on the input devices used. They found that stereo was beneficial for accuracy in the tasks they presented to users, but not for speed (Teather and Stuerzlinger 2007).

The interplay between 3D stereo and motion cues has been studied in very simple tasks. Ware and Mitchell found roughly an order of magnitude increase in the size of a graph that can be read at similar performance levels when 3D stereo viewing is available along with motion depth cues (Ware and Mitchell 2005). They concluded that any kind of motion improves performance and is more significant than stereo cues alone. Merritt et al. (1991) studied effects of motion parallax and stereoscopic 3D in a task to touch, in sequence, ten target sites embedded in a complex wire maze.

They found a large significant advantage for the 3D stereoscopic display condition vs. the 2D condition and a smaller significant advantage for the motion-parallax vs. the static condition.

2.2.4 Stereoscopic 3D Game Design

Creating graphical user interface (GUI) for stereoscopic 3D games is a difficult choice between visual comfort and effect. Schild et al. (2013) explored GUI design space for a stereoscopic 3D game in order to design comfortable game GUIs (e.g., menus and icons). Their results showed that in-game menus look best when displayed at the bottom of screen with a semi-transparent background. For referencing objects, they found that it is best to show the referencing information at the same depth as the object itself. Deepress3D is a flight game (Schild et al. 2014) which was custom designed keeping stereoscopic 3D viewing in mind. Their game design featured a stereoscopic specific GUI based on Schild et al. (2013) , no real depth illusions in graphics, and optimal parallax budget for stereoscopic viewing. Their results show that the users experienced an enhanced sense of presence in stereoscopic 3D viewing environment.

2.2.5 Negative Aspects of Stereoscopic 3D

While stereoscopic 3D has shown some positive benefits depending on the task, it also has shown to cause negative symptoms as well, such as eyestrain, headache, dizziness, and nausea (Hoffman et al. 2008; Howarth 2011; Lambooij et al. 2007). Stereoscopic 3D benefits can only be expected if the stereoscopic vision is not accompanied by distortions (e.g., contradicting depth cues, ghosting/cross-talk, exaggerated disparity) (Junyong You et al. 2010). There has been research on display techniques to reduce some of these symptoms (Bernhard et al. 2014; Colin Ware 1995).

2.3 Our Hypotheses

As discussed in related work, a previous study (Litwiller and LaViola 2011) for PC games showed that playing games in 3D stereo does not provide any significant performance benefits than with using a 2D display. However, this study used a traditional game controller (the Xbox 360 controller) as the interaction device and the games used were not designed with 3D stereo in mind. It has also been shown that an increase in body movement imposed, or allowed, by the game controller results in an increase in players engagement level (Bianchi-Berthouze et al. 2007; Lindley et al. 2008). In the cognitive science literature, it has been shown that there is a connection between actions and depth perception in that motor actions affect our perception of 3D space and objects (Wexler et al. 2005). Thus, allowing observers to physically act can drastically change the way they perceive the third dimension. Research has also shown that 3D stereo can be beneficial to user performance in certain, isolated tasks in the context of virtual reality and 3D user interfaces (Arthur et al. 1993; Hubona et al. 1999; Teather and Stuerzlinger 2007) using a 6° of freedom (6 DOF) input device. Based on these studies, we hypothesize that coupling 3D stereo with 3D spatial interaction using motion controllers in video games could lead to better user performance than with a 2D display and a motion controller.

To test the above hypotheses, we conducted a usability experiment with five PlayStation 3 3D games where participants played each game in either a 2D or 3D viewing mode using the PlayStation Move Controller. We examined both quantitative metrics based on each game's goals and tasks and qualitative metrics based on whether participants preferred playing the games in 3D and whether they perceived any benefits. Based on previous findings in related work and our analysis of the games, we hypothesize that users will gain a performance advantage when using 3D stereo coupled with a 3D interaction device over a 2D display coupled with the same 3D interaction device. In addition, we felt players would prefer playing games in 3D stereo coupled with the 3D interaction device (Move Controller) because it provides a more engaging user experience. Next, we will talk about our user experiment to examine the benefits of stereoscopic 3D.

2.4 User Evaluation Experiment

2.4.1 Selecting the Games for Our Experiment

We required a gaming environment that natively supported 3D stereo and 3D spatial interaction. At the time of this work, the only system that supported both these features was the PlayStation 3. We were able to find 16 games that supported both 3D stereo as well as the PlayStation Move controller and we examined them to see if playing them in 3D stereo provides any performance benefits. Some of these games had all their tasks in 2D so playing them in 3D stereo would not provide any benefit. Some games make use of the PlayStation Move controller for just a few tasks just to label the game as Move compatible. We removed all such games and we were left with just eight games. Out of those eight games, we removed three more games which we felt did not use 3D efficiently or had poor interface controls deterring any performance benefit. We were left with five games (see Fig. 2.1), Hustle Kings, Pain, The Fight: Lights out, Tumble, and Virtua Tennis 4, that could potentially provide performance benefits in a 3D stereo environment.

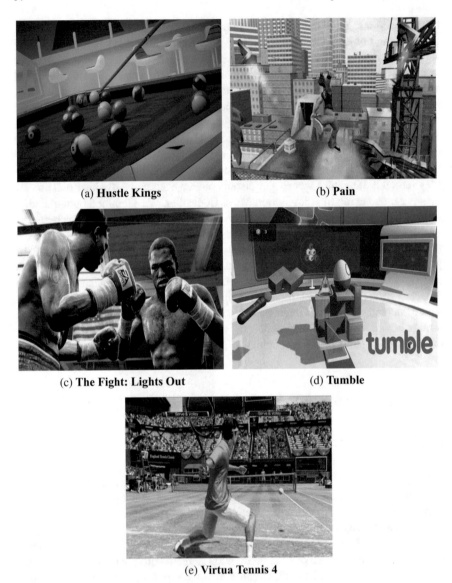

(a) **Hustle Kings**   (b) **Pain**

(c) **The Fight: Lights Out**   (d) **Tumble**

(e) **Virtua Tennis 4**

Fig. 2.1 Screenshots of the games used in stereoscopic 3D experiment

Hustle Kings is a pool table game which uses the Move controller as a cue stick used to hit the cue ball. The game displays an aiming line while adjusting the cue stick before taking a shot which indicates where the ball is going to hit. We disabled the aiming line so we could better judge how users performed with the coupling of 3D stereo and 3D spatial interaction.

Pain has a level "PainMotion: Skeet X3" which supports both 3D stereo as well as the Move controller. In this level, the player has to destroy all the incoming objects thrown at him or her by throwing a bomb before being hit by those objects. If the bomb misses any incoming object then the player will get hit and loses health and eventually dies. The Move controller is used to aim in the direction that the player wants to throw the bomb. We expected that the 3D stereo display and the Move controller together would let players perform better.

The Fight: Lights Out is a boxing game in which two Move controllers are used as two hands of the player. The player had to fight against an CPU controlled opponent. We thought that 3D stereo would help support better aiming when throwing punches at an opponent.

Tumble is a game which involves manipulation of 3D blocks of different shapes, materials, and sizes. This game involves many 3D selection and manipulation tasks. We chose a level called "Zone 2: Variety box" in which the player has to choose different objects and fit as many as possible on a table. The Move controller is used to pick and manipulate the objects. We felt that judgment of depth is critical when placing objects accurately so 3D stereo could be beneficial in this game.

Virtua Tennis 4 is a first person tennis game in which the Move controller is used as a tennis racquet. While playing this game, knowledge of distance of the tennis ball is necessary to time the racquet swing to hit the ball accurately. We thought that 3D stereo could be helpful in playing this game by achieving better ball hit accuracy. Moreover depth information could be used to hit the ball in different directions while playing.

2.4.2 Participants and Equipment

Fifty participants (38 males and 12 females ranging in age from 18 to 34 with a mean age of 23.04) were recruited from the University of Central Florida. A modified version of Terlecki and Newcombe's Video Game Experience survey (Terlecki and Newcombe 2005) was used as a pre-questionnaire in which they answered questions about their previous gaming experience. The survey was modified to include questions related to previous experience with the PlayStation 3, the Move Controller, and the stereo 3D games used for the study. Of the 50 participants, 18 were ranked as beginners (10 in stereo group and 8 in non-stereo group), 23 as intermediate (9 in stereo group and 14 in non-stereo group), and 9 as advanced (6 in stereo group and 3 in non-stereo group). Since there were only a few advanced users, we decided to combine intermediate and advanced categories into one category called expert users. The experiment duration ranged from 75 to 90 min depending on how long participants took to complete the tasks presented to them in the games and how much time was spent on the questionnaire. All participants were paid $10 for their time.

Fig. 2.2 The experimental setup used a Samsung 50 inch DLP 3D HDTV, PlayStation 3 game console, PlayStation Move controller, and a Mitsubishi 3D adapter (to convert the HDMI 1.4a 3D signal to a DLP 3D signal). These are all commodity hardware components

The 3D setup (see Fig. 2.2) used for the study consisted of a PlayStation 3 with PlayStation Eye camera, PlayStation Move Controllers, Mitsubishi 3D adapter (to convert HDMI 1.4a 3D signal to DLP 3D signal), Samsung 50 inch DLP 3D HDTV, and Optoma (DLP Link) active shutter glasses. For the 2D display condition, the Mitsubishi 3D adapter was not used and PlayStation 3 rendered graphics in 2D.

2.4.3   Experimental Task

The participants were given tasks to play through levels of the five games that were selected for this study. For each game, they were presented with a task specific to that game and a goal for completing each task. Participants played these games in random order (counter-balanced Latin Squares design) with three attempts for each game.

Hustle Kings: The participants played "Free Play" with no opponent. Their task was to pocket as many balls (with no constraint on the ball color) as possible in six shots (including the first hit). The table was reset after each attempt (consisting of 6 shots).

Pain: In this game participants played "PainMotion: Skeet X3" and their task was to destroy as many objects (thrown at them) as possible by throwing a bomb. The better they play the longer they survive in the game.

The Fight: Lights Out: The participants played "First Fight" using two Move controllers. Their task was to fight and defeat the opponent.

Tumble: The participants played "Zone 2: Variety Box" where the task was to put as many blocks as possible on a table in the game. The size of the table was limited so they had to cleverly arrange the objects on the table in order to stack other objects on top of them. The maximum time limit for each attempt was ten minutes. The time limit of 10 min was determined during pilot testing with this game. The moderator kept track of time taken by participants for each attempt.

Virtua Tennis 4: The participants had to play "Motion Play" using the move controller as a tennis racquet. Participants played three matches against a randomly chosen opponent. The moderator kept track of score and time taken by participants for each attempt.

2.4.4 Design and Procedure

Our study design was based, in part, on the study done by Litwiller and LaViola (2011). We chose a between subjects design, to avoid any effects of learning on user performance, where the independent variable was display mode (2D display or 3D stereo display) and the dependent variables were the various scoring metrics used in each game. We wanted some additional information about the use of 3D stereo in video games for those who played the games in the 2D display condition. Thus, we chose to have those participants who were in the 2D display condition, pick one game to try in 3D stereo to gather their reactions.

In order to group the participants into expertise levels based on the pre-questionnaire data, we scored the questionnaire by assigning points to each question. Particular questions were given more points based on how the results fit within the context of our experimental setup. For example, participants who owned gaming consoles and have been playing regularly were considered to have a higher expertise level. We then used the raw scores from adding up the points for each question to group the participants into the appropriate category. Both the quantitative and qualitative data was explored collectively as well as according to the two groupings (beginners and experts).

2.4.4.1 Quantitative and Qualitative Metrics

For each game, we tracked quantitative data that we felt was a good indication of how well the user performed. Quantitative metrics are summarized in Table 2.1.

In Hustle Kings, we kept a record of the number of balls pocketed in each run consisting of 6 shots. In Pain, player survival time and bomb throwing accuracy (calculated from number of hits and throws reported by the game) were tracked as performance metrics. In The Fight, calories burned and punch accuracy (reported by

Table 2.1 Summary of metrics for each game. The metrics are used to quantify how users in the 2D and 3D display groups performed

Game	Metric
Hustle kings	Number of balls pocketed
Pain	Time accuracy of throws
The fight: lights out	Calorie count accuracy of punches
Tumble	Time taken number of blocks used
Virtua Tennis 4	Match won or lost

the game) were tracked as performance metrics. In Tumble, the number of blocks used and level completion time with a maximum limit of 10 min per trial were tracked. In Virtua Tennis 4, match outcome (lost or won) was the only performance metric.

For qualitative data, all participants filled out an immersion questionnaire (Jennett et al. 2008) (see Table 2.2) upon completion of all trials of each game. The questionnaire was modified to include two questions about controllers to determine

Table 2.2 Post-game Questionnaire. Participants answered these questions on a 7 point Likert scale after playing each game. We used this data for qualitative analysis

Postgame Questions	
Q1	To what extent did the game hold your attention?
Q2	How much effort did you put into playing the game?
Q3	Did you feel you were trying your best?
Q4	To what extent did you lose track of time?
Q5	Did you feel the urge to see what was happening around you?
Q6	To what extent you enjoyed playing the game, rather than something you were just doing?
Q7	To what extent did you find the game challenging?
Q8	How well do you think you performed in the game?
Q9	To what extent did you feel emotionally attached to the game?
Q10	To what extent did you enjoy the graphics and the imagery?
Q11	How much would you say you enjoyed playing the game?
Q12	Would you like to play the game again?
Q13	Was use of Move Controller helpful in playing the game?
Q14	To what extent your arm was tired after playing the game?
Q15	DualShock 3 would be a better choice to play this game?

Table 2.3 3D Stereo Questionnaire. Participants responded to statements 1-4 on a 7 point Likert scale. Questions 5–10 were multiple choice and open ended questions to gauge the users perception of the effects of 3D stereo. In question 11, each symptom had a 7 point Likert scale to indicate the extent of each symptom ranging from not at all to very much so

3D Stereo Questions	
Q1	3D stereo improved the overall experience of the game
Q2	I would choose to play in 3D stereo over normal viewing
Q3	I felt that stereo enhanced the sense of engagement I felt
Q4	3D stereo is a necessity for my future game experiences
Q5	Did 3D stereo help you perform better in the games?
Q6	Which games did it help you in?
Q7	How did it help you in those games?
Q8	Did 3D stereo decrease your performance in the games?
Q9	Which games did it decrease your performance in?
Q10	How did it decrease your performance in those games?
Q11	Did you feel any symptoms from viewing the games in stereo (eye strain, headache, dizziness, nausea)?

the helpfulness of the Move controller and the traditional controller (DualShock 3). Another question was included to determine if the player experienced arm fatigue from using the Move controller. Responses were measured on a 7 point Likert scale (1 = most negative response, 7 = most positive response). Upon completion of all experimental tasks participants were given a survey to determine how 3D stereo affected their gaming experience (see Table 2.3) and whether they preferred to play the games in 3D stereo and if 3D stereo helped or hurt their performance.

2.4.4.2 Procedure

The experiment began with the participant seated in front of the TV and the moderator seated aside. Participants were given a standard consent form that explained the study. They were then given a pre-questionnaire that focused on their gaming expertise. Participants were then presented with the games in random order (Latin Squares design). Half the participants played the games in 2D display mode (control group) and half played in 3D stereo (experimental group). The moderator would present the game and give instructions to the participant as to what they needed to accomplish in the game and what their goals were. They were also instructed on how to use the PlayStation Move controller. During the experiment, the moderator recorded quantitative data using scores from the games and a stopwatch for timing information. After each game, the participant filled out a post-questionnaire with questions about their experiences with the game. If the participants played the five games in the 2D display group, they then selected one game to play in 3D stereo. All participants were given a final post-questionnaire about their experiences with the 3D stereo display. In the next section, we will discuss the results of our experiment.

2.5   Results and Analysis

We broke up the participants in each display group (3D and 2D group) into beginners (8 participants in the 2D display group, 10 participants in the 3D stereo group) and expert gamers (17 participants in the 2D display group, 15 participants in the 3D stereo group). To analyze the performance data, a two-way ANOVA was conducted that examined the effect of game-play expertise (EXP), beginner or expert, and the display mode (DM), 2D or 3D, on the user performance (see Table 2.1 for metrics used for each game). We did a post-hoc analysis using independent sample t-tests. We used Holm's sequential Bonferroni adjustment to correct for type I errors (Sture Holm 1979) and the Kolmogorov-Smirnov test to make sure our data is parametric. We also wanted to see whether there was learning taking place in the form of game play improvement. We looked at the improvement in the performance measures for each game from the first user run to their last run using a repeated measures ANOVA. Finally we wanted to look at the participant's perception of their performance through the post questionnaires. To analyze this Likert scale data, we used the Mann-Whitney test. For all of our statistical measures, we used $\alpha = 0.05$.

2.5.1   Hustle Kings

No statistically significant differences were found between overall mean performance scores of the two display mode groups (see Table 2.4 and Fig. 2.3). However, when we looked at the individual runs for the expert gamers, we did find a significant difference ($t_{30} = -2.79$, $p < 0.01$) between the balls pocketed in their last attempt, with the 3D stereo group pocketing an average of 2.93 balls ($\sigma = 1.33$) compared to an average of 1.65 balls ($\sigma = 1.27$) for the 2D display group. In terms of score improvement, beginners had no significant score improvements from the first attempt to the last attempt for both the 3D display ($F_{2,8} = 1.964$, $p = 0.169$)

Table 2.4 Two-way ANOVA analysis for Hustle Kings. No significance was found

Source	Average balls pocketed
DM	$F_{1,46} = 1.491$, $p = 0.228$
EXP	$F_{1,46} = 0.348$, $p = 0.558$
EXP × DM	$F_{1,46} = 2.374$, $p = 0.130$

Fig. 2.3 Hustle Kings: Differences in average number of balls pocketed between the 2D and 3D groups in the two gamer categories. Expert gamers did better in 3D mode

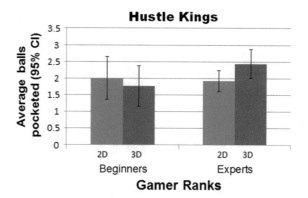

and the 2D display ($F_{2,6} = 0.467$, $p = 0.637$) groups. For expert gamers, the 3D stereo group ($F_{2,13} = 3.530$, $p < 0.05$) significantly improved the average number of balls pocketed from 2.00 in the first run to 2.93 in the third run (46.5% improvement). No significant score improvements were found for the 2D display group ($F_{2,15} = 0.888$, $p = 0.421$).

From the qualitative data, beginners in the 2D display group ($\bar{x} = 6.62$, $\sigma = 0.517$) enjoyed the graphics and imagery significantly more ($Z = -2.563$, $p < 0.05$) than the 3D stereo group ($\bar{x} = 5.4$, $\sigma = 1.173$). There were no significant differences in any of the questions for expert gamers. Overall, participants thought that the Dual-Shock 3 controller would not be a good choice for this game ($\bar{x} = 3.06$, $\sigma = 2.20$).

2.5.2 Pain

Table 2.5 shows the 2-way ANOVA analysis for completion time and accuracy. Expert gamers performed significantly better than beginners in terms of time ($t_{48} = -4.029$, $p < 0.025$) and accuracy ($t_{48} = -5.609$, $p < 0.025$). For both beginners and expert gamers, the 3D stereo group performed slightly better than the 2D display group (see Fig. 2.4), but the differences were not significant. For score improvement, beginners showed no significant improvement in either the 2D display group ($F_{2,6} = 0.008$, $p = 0.992$) or the 3D stereo group ($F_{2,8} = 1.444$, $p = 0.262$). For expert gamers, we did not find any significant improvements from their first attempt to their last attempt in the 2D display group ($F_{2,15} = 0.513$, $p = 0.604$) or the 3D stereo group ($F_{2,13} = 1.066$, $p = 0.358$). However, we did find significant improvements from the first attempt to the second attempt in the 3D stereo group ($F_{1,14} = 5.202$, $p < 0.05$) with no such significant differences in the 2D display group ($F_{1,16} = 1.546$, $p = 0.232$). The 3D stereo group improved their accuracy from 58.15% ($\sigma = 13.06$) in their first attempt to 61.73% ($\sigma = 12.03$) in their second attempt which is a 6.15% improvement.

Table 2.5 Two-way ANOVA analysis for Pain. Difference due to game play expertise was significant

Source	Time	Accuracy
DM	$F_{1,46} = 1.702, p = 0.199$	$F_{1,46} = 2.251, p = 0.140$
EXP	$F_{1,46} = 17.109, p < 0.01$	$F_{1,46} = 32.936, p < 0.01$
DG $\times$ EXP	$F_{1,46} = 0.313, p = 0.579$	$F_{1,46} = 0.000, p = 0.992$

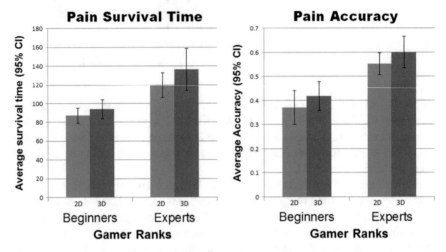

Fig. 2.4 Pain: Differences in survival time and accuracy between the 2D and 3D groups in the two gamer categories. Players survived slightly longer in 3D stereo in both gamer ranks. People had slightly more hit accuracy in 3D stereo compared to the 2D display group

For the questionnaire data, people thought that the DualShock 3 controller would not have been a good choice for this game ($\bar{x} = 2.80, \sigma = 2.27$). For beginners, participants in the 2D display group ($\bar{x} = 6.50, \sigma = 0.755$) put significantly more effort ($Z = -2.002, p < 0.05$) into playing the game than the 3D stereo group ($\bar{x} = 5.5, \sigma = 1.08$) while the expert gamers did not show any significance for effort between the 2D and 3D stereo groups ($Z = -1.659, p = 0.097$). All other Likert scale questions between the two groups were not significant.

2.5.3 The Fight: Lights Out

No statistically significant differences were found (see Table 2.6 and Fig. 2.5) based on display group or game play expertise. In terms of score improvement, there was no significant improvement for beginners from their first to the last attempt in the 2D display group ($F_{2,6} = 1.110, p = 0.357$). However, we did find significant improvements in the 3D stereo group ($F_{2,8} = 4.870, p < 0.05$) . The beginner 3D stereo

Table 2.6 Two-way ANOVA analysis for The Fight. No significance was found

Source	Calories	Accuracy
DM	$F_{1,46} = 0.230, p = 0.634$	$F_{1,46} = 0.58, p = 0.811$
EXP	$F_{1,46} = 1.599, p = 0.212$	$F_{1,46} = 0.320, p = 0.574$
DG × EXP	$F_{1,46} = 0.273, p = 0.604$	$F_{1,46} = 0.033, p = 0.857$

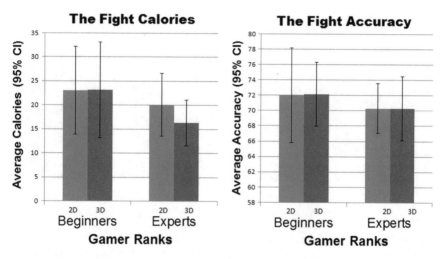

Fig. 2.5 The Fight: Differences in calories burned and hit accuracy between the 2D and 3D groups in the two gamer categories. Expert players burned more calories in 2D display group. Beginners were more accurate than expert gamers

group improved their accuracy from 66.4% ($\sigma = 12.08$) in their first attempt to 74.0% ($\sigma = 5.37$) in their last attempt, a 11.44% improvement. In the case of expert gamers, there were significant improvements in accuracy for both the 2D display group ($F_{2,15} = 11.662, p < 0.05$) and the 3D stereo group ($F_{2,13} = 5.511, p < 0.05$) from their first to last attempt. The 2D display group improved their accuracy from 64.29% ($\sigma = 7.74$) to 73.05% ($\sigma = 9.90$), a 13.62% improvement and the 3D stereo group improved their accuracy from 67.53% ($\sigma = 9.24$) to 73.80% ($\sigma = 8.97$), a 9.28% improvement. Both groups felt their arms got tired after playing this game ($\bar{x} = 5.58, \sigma = 1.72$). For beginners, the game held their attention significantly more ($Z = -1.954, p < 0.05$) with the 2D display group ($\bar{x} = 7.0, \sigma = 0$) group than with the 3D stereo group ($\bar{x} = 6.3, \sigma = 1.05$).

2.5.4 Tumble

Table 2.7 shows the results from the 2-way ANOVA analysis for Tumble. For beginners, the 3D stereo group ($\bar{x} = 15.333, \sigma = 2.504$) performed significantly better

Table 2.7 Two-way ANOVA analysis for Tumble. Significance in the number of blocks used

Source	Time	Blocks used
DM	$F_{1,46} = 1.125, p = 0.294$	$F_{1,46} = 4.106, p < 0.05$
EXP	$F_{1,46} = 1.497, p = 0.227$	$F_{1,46} = 13.706, p < 0.01$
DG $\times$ EXP	$F_{1,46} = 0.601, p = 0.442$	$F_{1,46} = 2.682, p = 0.108$

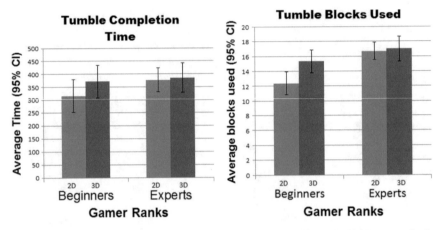

Fig. 2.6 Tumble: Differences in number of blocks used between the 2D and 3D groups in the two gamer categories. Beginners performed significantly better in 3D stereo, while there was no significant difference (between the 2D and 3D display groups) for expert gamers

($t_{16} = -2.628$, $p < 0.025$) than the 2D display group ($\bar{x} = 12.375$, $\sigma = 2.19$) for average number of blocks used. For expert gamers, no significant differences between average completion times ($t_{30} = -0.233$, $p = 0.818$) or average number of blocks used ($t_{30} = -0.306$, $p = 0.762$) was found between groups (see Fig. 2.6 for plots).

For score improvement, beginners showed no significant improvements from their first attempt to last attempt in the number of blocks used for either the 3D stereo group ($F_{2,8} = 0.507$, $p = 0.611$) or the 2D display group ($F_{2,6} = 1.661$, $p = 0.225$). However, for expert gamers, we found significant improvements for blocks used in the 2D display group ($F_{2,15} = 5.759$, $p < 0.05$) but not in the 3D stereo group ($F_{2,13} = 0.781$, $p = 0.468$). The 2D display group improved the number of blocks used from 14.64 ($\sigma = 4.51$) in their first attempt to 18.94 ($\sigma = 3.36$) in their last attempt, a 29.37% improvement.

When we analyzed the qualitative data we found significant differences for many questions. For beginners, participants felt they performed significantly better ($Z = -2.093$, $p < 0.05$) in the 3D stereo group ($\bar{x} = 5.900$, $\sigma = 1.100$) than in the 2D display group ($\bar{x} = 4.250$, $\sigma = 1.752$). Beginners in the 2D display group ($\bar{x} = 2.875$, $\sigma = 2.167$) felt the DualShock 3 controller would be a significantly better choice ($Z = -2.438$, $p < 0.05$) for this game than beginners in the 3D stereo group ($\bar{x} = 1.100$, $\sigma = 0.316$). For expert gamers, Tumble held significantly more

Table 2.8 Ordinal logistic regression analysis for Virtua Tennis 4. No significance was found

Source	Average number of wins
DM	$\chi^2(1) = 2.098, p = 0.147$
EXP	$\chi^2(1) = 1.792, p = 0.181$
DG $\times$ EXP	$\chi^2(1) = 2.118, p = 0.146$

attention ($Z = -2.723$, $p < 0.05$) of the 3D stereo group ($\bar{x} = 6.800$, $\sigma = 0.414$) than the 2D display group ($\bar{x} = 5.823$, $\sigma = 1.236$). The 3D stereo group ($\bar{x} = 1.733$, $\sigma = 1.579$) felt significantly less distracted ($Z = -2.676$, $p < 0.05$) than the 2D group ($\bar{x} = 3.705$, $\sigma = 2.114$) and did feel the need to look around to see what was happening around them. The 3D stereo group ($\bar{x} = 6.466$, $\sigma = 0.990$) enjoyed the game significantly more ($Z = -1.976$, $p < 0.05$) than the 2D display group ($\bar{x} = 5.647$, $\sigma = 1.411$) as well. When asked whether the participants would play the game again, the 3D stereo group ($\bar{x} = 6.266$, $\sigma = 1.387$) showed significantly more interest ($Z = -2.660$, $p < 0.05$) than the 2D display group ($\bar{x} = 4.764$, $\sigma = 1.953$).

2.5.5   Virtua Tennis 4

In this case, the average number of wins is not normally distributed so we used ordinal logistic regression analysis, with display mode (DM) and gaming expertise (EXP) as predictors, for between subject effects and Friedman test for learning effects. No statistically significant differences were found (see Table 2.8 for Wald's-χ^2 test results). No statistical significance was found between any group (beginners 2D vs 3D stereo and expert 2D vs 3D stereo) in terms of score improvement. For beginners, participants in the 2D display group ($\bar{x} = 6.00$, $\sigma = 2.07$) thought they performed significantly better ($Z = -2.155$, $p < 0.05$) than the participants in the 3D stereo group($\bar{x} = 4.1$, $\sigma = 2.23$). For expert gamers, we did not find any statistical significance in the qualitative data.

2.5.6   Stereoscopic 3D Questions

Out of the 25 participants in the 2D display group, one chose to play Hustle Kings, one chose to play Pain, five chose to play The Fight, six chose Tumble, and 12 chose to play Virtua Tennis 4. The participants who played Hustle Kings and Pain thought that 3D stereo helped them. All five participants who played The Fight thought that 3D stereo helped them. Five out of six participants who played Tumble thought that 3D stereo helped them while eight out of 12 people who played tennis thought that 3D stereo helped them.

Out of the 25 participants from the 3D stereo group that played all the games in stereo, 19 participants thought that it gave them an advantage in at least one of the games, 12 participants thought that it decreased their performance in at least one of the games and three participants thought that it did not help nor decrease their performance in any way. No participants in this group thought that 3D stereo decreased their performance in Tumble.

All the participants filled out a questionnaire about their 3D stereo experience, responding to questions Q1-Q5 on a 7 point Likert scale (1 = Strongly Disagree, 7 = Strongly Agree) (see Table 2.3). Participants agreed that 3D stereo improved their overall gaming experience ($\bar{x} = 6.00, \sigma = 1.44$), they would choose to play video games in 3D stereo over the 2D display ($\bar{x} = 5.76, \sigma = 1.90$), and that it enhanced the sense of engagement they felt ($\bar{x} = 5.68, \sigma = 1.89$). However, some participants did not think it was a necessity for their future game experiences ($\bar{x} = 4.72, \sigma = 2.10$). None of participants felt any significant cybersickness symptoms such as eye strain ($\bar{x} = 1.90, \sigma = 1.40$), headache ($\bar{x} = 1.38, \sigma = 0.77$), dizziness ($\bar{x} = 1.56, \sigma = 1.28$), or nausea ($\bar{x} = 1.08, \sigma = 0.34$). When we divided the data between the 2D display group and 3D stereo group, we found that the 2D display group ($\bar{x} = 6.48, \sigma = 0.871$) felt that 3D stereo significantly improved their overall experience ($Z = -2.125, p < 0.05$) compared to the 3D stereo group ($\bar{x} = 5.52, \sigma = 1.73$). When broken down based on gamer ranks, there was no significant difference ($Z = -0.786, p = 0.432$) between groups. However, for expert gamers, the 2D display group ($\bar{x} = 6.47, \sigma = 0.943$) felt 3D stereo improved their overall experience significantly more ($Z = -2.029, p < 0.05$) than the 3D stereo group ($\bar{x} = 5.4, \sigma = 1.63$).

2.6 Discussion

From our quantitative data analysis, we can see that 3D stereo provided significant performance advantages for expert gamers for the last attempt in Hustle Kings and for beginners for Tumble in general. The other games tested showed no significant performance benefits compared with a 2D display. When participants interacted with only one object at a time with a more or less static background environment (e.g., aiming a cue ball or putting blocks on a table in 3D space) significant performance benefits occurred for 3D stereo over the 2D display. However, no significant user performance benefits were found in tasks where the scene was complex (e.g., a fight scene with player moving around) or dynamic (e.g., many incoming objects in Pain or tracking a moving ball in Tennis). Note that similar results were found in Litwiller and LaViola (2011) in terms of games with complex and dynamic scenes not showing user performance benefits in 3D stereo compared to a 2D display. Additionally with some games (e.g., The Fight and Virtua Tennis 4), users need to move around with the 3D glasses which can cause the 3D glasses to flicker because of signal loss between the 3D sync signal from the TV and the glasses. This flicker could also cause distraction and affect user performance. We believe that this result supports prior findings (Arthur et al. 1993; McMahan et al. 2006; Teather and Stuerzlinger 2007) in the virtual reality and 3D user interface communities that 3D stereo can provide user performance benefits for isolated object position and manipulation tasks in static scenes.

Another interesting finding from the quantitative results is based on performance between beginners and expert gamers in both the 2D display and 3D stereo groups. For example, in Tumble, beginners showed significant performance benefits with 3D stereo compared to the 2D display but not expert gamers while the opposite is true for Hustle Kings. For Tumble, we believe different depth cues coupled with game experience is one of the reasons for this result. In Tumble, shadows are present under the blocks as an additional depth cue indicating their position and orientation in 3D space. Shadows have been shown to be helpful in 3D tasks (Hubona et al. 1999) and are a common depth cue in video games. We theorize when presented with two depth cues (e.g., 3D stereo and shadows), expert gamers would be more used to using shadows as a tool to judge depth since it is common in their game play experience, while beginners indicated that 3D stereo served as a better depth cue than shadows. Thus, all things being equal, we believe beginners made better use of 3D stereo than the expert gamers because the expert gamers focused on shadows, a depth cue that was common to both conditions. However, more work is needed to verify this postulate.

For Hustle Kings, we believe the controller itself played a role in user performance between beginners and expert gamers. It has been shown that interaction devices significantly affect user performance (McMahan et al. 2006). Interacting with the pool cue in Hustle Kings was sensitive using the PlayStation Move Controller, making it challenging to do fine grained manipulation. We observed many cases where beginners had difficulty controlling the cue stick while the expert gamers tended to have more control and more patience with the interface. Coupled with 3D stereo, the expert gamers were able to achieve better performance in their last attempt with this game.

While examining the learning effects (e.g., score improvement across attempts in each game), we noticed that 3D stereo helped participants improve their scores in games which provided an advantage from added depth perception. The Fight, Pain, and Hustle Kings are notable examples. What this result shows is that the 3D stereo group, especially for the expert gamers, were able to catch up to the performance levels of their 2D display counterparts. For Tumble and Virtua Tennis 4, performance improvement across runs was not significant. In Tumble, the 3D stereo group already started at a higher level than the 2D display group and did not improve much from attempt to attempt. However, the 2D display expert gamer group improved their performance with repeated attempts and caught up with 3D stereo group. It is also interesting to note that none of the beginners in the 2D display group were able to significantly improve their scores in any of the games tested.

User fatigue could also have been an important factor during these experiments. The PlayStation Move controller requires user motion while playing which can possibly cause arm fatigue, depending on the kind of motion. This may have suppressed learning effects to some extent because after each trial the user's arm fatigue possibly increases; in some cases reducing performance in the next trial. Pain is an example in which we find significant improvements from first to second trial but there were no improvements from second to third trial. Surprisingly, 3D stereo fatigue did not appear to play a role in the experiment as we did not notice any significant side effects (headache, eye strain, dizziness, and nausea) of 3D viewing in any of the participants during game play.

In the qualitative data we found some significant differences in the two user groups (2D vs 3D stereo). We noticed that 3D stereo is perceived to be more enjoyable and immersive than 2D viewing only for the games which provide an overall advantage using 3D stereo (e.g., Tumble), but no significant differences were found in the other games we tested. In general, almost all participants were not familiar with the games we used for our study, so most of them were excited to play using the PlayStation Move controller with 3D stereo acting as a secondary factor in their game play experience. This may be the reason that, qualitatively, they perceived similar game play experiences, no matter what group they were in. Most people liked the 3D stereo game play experience but some users felt they were so accustomed to playing on a 2D display that the 3D effect distracted them.

Additionally, our qualitative data indicates that 3D stereo is perceived to be more enjoyable and immersive than 2D viewing only for the games which provide an advantage in 3D stereo. This outcome contradicts previous findings, which reported preference for 3D stereo although no advantages in performance were found (Litwiller and LaViola 2011; Rajae-Joordens 2008). These results lead to our conclusion that games need to be particularly designed to allow a benefit in performance from stereoscopic vision. As part of such a design, using a 3D motion controller as a game controller can have a positive impact. A starting point in game design, based on the game Tumble, could be to isolate depth precision tasks. The stereoscopic effect could be used alongside other depth cues to create game conflicts and for balancing tasks, an approach also described in Schild and Masuch (2011). Based on the above findings and on our observations, we recommend game designers to

- Utilize relatively simple scenes or static environments where interaction is focused on isolated tasks to provide user performance benefits with 3D stereo. This approach can help to avoid user distraction.
- Try to emphasize the stereo effect, showing how to use it in gameplay, especially expert users who may not take it into account.
- Provide a way to control the sensitivity of the controller to make it a more enjoyable user experience.
- Avoid requiring a lot of user motion in front of the display to avoid any sync signal loss issues with active 3D stereo glasses and to reduce geometric errors when leaving the sweet spot for 3D effect. Alternatively provide tracked stereo or RF signal based sync.

2.7 Conclusion

For the first time, we observed a positive impact of 3D stereo on gaming performance, which seems to be related to 3D interaction. However, our results reveal that performance in 3D interaction gaming does not automatically benefit from 3D stereoscopic vision. Interestingly, 3D stereo can specifically provide a significant performance advantage over 2D vision in rather isolated tasks, when users are manipulating one object at a time and when a scene is more or less static. In simple scenes impact of 3D stereo on performance is much greater than in complex games where many dynamic factors (camera perspective, enemy behavior, and other animated elements) around the interacting object influence the course of the game. A third important finding is that game expertise has the potential to nullify this effect, as observed in the Tumble game. A possible reason is that gamers may have learned to rely on other cues than binocular disparity (e.g., on shadows and lighting). Hence, beginners are more open to using new visual cues and thus benefit more from using 3D stereoscopic vision.

So far we have explored potential benefits of stereoscopic 3D in games. In the next chapter, we will explore benefits of head tracking in games using a systematic experiment.

References

Arns L, Cruz-Neira C, Cook D (1999) The benefits of statistical visualization in an immersive environment. In: Proceedings of the IEEE virtual reality VR. IEEE Computer Society, Washington, DC, p 88

Arthur KW, Booth KS, Ware C (1993) Evaluating 3D task performance for fish tank virtual worlds. ACM Trans Inf Syst 11(3):239–265

Bernhard M et al (2014) The effects of fast disparity adjustment in gazecontrolled stereoscopic applications. In: Proceedings of the symposium on eye tracking research and applications. ETRA '14. ACM, Safety Harbor, Florida, pp 111–118. ISBN: 978-1-4503-2751-0. https://doi.org/10.1145/2578153.2578169

Bianchi-Berthouze N, Kim WW, Patel D (2007) Does body movement engage you more in digital game play? and why? In: Proceedings of the 2nd international conference on affective computing and intelligent interaction, vol 4738. pp 102–113

Fujimoto M, Ishibashi Y (2005) The Effect of stereoscopic viewing of a virtual space on a networked game using haptic media. In: Proceedings of the ACM SIGCHI international conference on advances in computer entertainment. ACM, New York, NY, pp 317–320

Grossman T, Balakrishnan R (2006) An evaluation of depth perception on volumetric displays. In: Proceedings of the working conference on advanced visual interfaces. AVI '06. ACM, Venezia, Italy, pp 193–200. ISBN: 1-59593-353-0. https://doi.org/10.1145/1133265.1133305

Gruchalla K (2004) Immersive well-path editing: investigating the added value of immersion. In: Proceedings of the IEEE virtual reality. pp 157–164. https://doi.org/10.1109/VR.2004.1310069

Hoffman DM et al (2008) Vergence-accommodation conflicts hinder visual performance and cause visual fatigue. J Vis 8(3):33

Holm Sture (1979) A simple sequentially rejective multiple test procedure. Scandinavian J Stat 6(2):65–70

Howarth PA (2011) Potential hazards of viewing 3D stereoscopic television, cinema and computer games: a review. Ophthalmic Physiol Opt : J B Coll Ophthalmic Opt (Optometrists) 31(2):111–122

Hubona GS et al (1999) The relative contributions of stereo, lighting, and background scenes in promoting 3D depth visualization. ACM Trans Comput-Human Interact 6(3):214–242

Jennett C et al (2008) Measuring and defining the experience of immersion in games. Int J Human-Comput Stud 66(9):641–661

Jin Z et al (2007) Evaluating the usability of an auto-stereoscopic display. In: Human-computer interaction. Interaction platforms and techniques, vol 4551. Springer, Berlin, Heidelberg, pp 605–614. ISBN: 978-3-540-73106-1

Jones JA et al (2008) The effects of virtual reality, augmented reality, and motion parallax on egocentric depth perception. In: Proceedings of applied perception in graphics and visualization. ACM, New York, NY, pp 9–14

Kickuth R et al (2002) Stereoscopic 3D CT vs standard 3D CT in the classification of acetabular fractures: an experimental study. British J Radiol 25:422–427

Lindley SE, Le Couteur J, Berthouze NL (2008) Stirring up experience through movement in game play: effects on engagement and social behaviour. In: Proceeding of the twenty-sixth annual SIGCHI conference on Human factors in computing systems. ACM, New York, NY, USA, pp 511–514

Litwiller T, LaViola JJ Jr. (2011) Evaluating the benefits of 3D stereo in modern video games. In: Proceedings of the SIGCHI conference on human factors in computing systems. CHI'11. ACM, New York, NY, USA, pp 2345–2354. https://doi.org/10.1145/1978942.1979286

Marc TM, Lambooij WA (2007) IJsselsteijn, and Ingrid Heynderickx. Visual discomfort in stereoscopic displays: a review, vol 6490. pp 64900I–64900I-13. https://doi.org/10.1117/12.705527

McMahan RP et al (2006) Separating the effects of level of immersion and 3D interaction techniques. In: Proceedings of the ACM symposium on virtual reality software and technology. ACM, New York, NY, pp 108–111

Menendez RG, Bernard JE (2001) Flight simulation in synthetic. Aerosp Electron Syst Mag IEEE 16(9):19–23

Merritt JO, Cole RE, Ikehara C (1991) A rapid-sequential-positioning task for evaluating motion parallax and stereoscopic 3D cues in teleoperator displays. In: Systems, man, and cybernetics. 1991 ieee international conference on decision aiding for complex systems, conference proceedings, 2 Oct 1991. pp 1041–1046

Munz Y et al (2004) The benefits of stereoscopic vision in robotic-assisted performance on bench models. In: Surgical Endoscopy. pp 611–616

Rosemarie JE (2008) Rajae-Joordens. Measuring experiences in gaming and TV applications. In: Probing experience, vol 8. Philips Re. Springer Netherlands, pp 77–90. ISBN: 978-1-4020-6593-4

Schild J et al (2013) Creating and analyzing stereoscopic 3D graphical user interfaces in digital games. In: Proceedings of the SIGCHI conference on human factors in computing systems. CHI '13. ACM, Paris, France, pp 169–178. ISBN: 978-1-4503-1899-0. https://doi.org/10.1145/2470654.2470678

Schild J, LaViola JJ Jr, Masuch M (2012) Understanding user experience in stereoscopic 3D games. In: Proceedings of the SIGCHI conference on human factors in computing systems. CHI '12. ACM, New York, NY, USA, pp 89–98. https://doi.org/10.1145/2207676.2207690

Schild J, LaViola JJ Jr, Masuch M (2014) Altering gameplay behavior using stereoscopic 3D vision-based video game design. In: Proceedings of the SIGCHI conference on human factors in computing systems. CHI '14. ACM, Toronto, Ontario, Canada, pp 207–216. ISBN:978-1-4503-2473-1. https://doi.org/10.1145/2556288.2557283

Schild J, Masuch M (2011) Fundamentals of stereoscopic 3D game design. In: ICEC, international federation for information processing. pp 155–160

Teather RJ, Stuerzlinger W (2007) Guidelines for 3D positioning techniques. In: Proceedings of the 2007 conference on future play. ACM, New York, NY, pp 61–68

Terlecki MS, Newcombe NS (2005) How important is the digital divide? The relation of computer and videogame usage gender differences in mental rotation ability. Sex Roles 53:433–441

Treadgold M et al (2001) What do you think you're doing? measuring perception in fish tank virtual reality. In: Proceedings of the international conference on computer graphics. IEEE Computer Society, Washington, DC, p 325

Ware C (1995) Dynamic stereo displays. In: Proceedings of the SIGCHI conference on human factors in computing systems. CHI '95. ACM Press/Addison-Wesley Publishing Co., Denver, Colorado, USA, pp 310–316. ISBN: 0-201-84705-1. https://doi.org/10.1145/223904.223944

Ware C, Franck G (1996) Evaluating stereo and motion cues for visualizing information nets in three dimensions. ACM Trans Graph 15(2):121–140

Ware C, Lowther K (1997) Selection using a one-eyed cursor in a fish tank VR environment. ACM Trans Comput-Human Interact 4(4):309–322

Ware C, Mitchell P (2005) Reevaluating stereo and motion cues for visualizing graphs in three dimensions. In: Proceedings of applied perception in graphics and visualization. ACM, New York, NY, pp 51–58

Wexler M, van Boxtel JJA (2005) Depth perception by the active observer. In: Trends in cognitive sciences 9.9. pp 431–438. ISSN: 1364-6613

Yamauchi Y, Shinohara K (2005) Effect of binocular stereopsis on surgical manipulation performance and fatigue when using a stereoscopic endoscope. In: Medicine meets virtual reality 13: the magical next becomes the medical now, vol 111. IOS Press, pp 611–614. ISBN: 978-1-58603-498-6

You J et al (2010) Quality of visual experience for 3D presentation -stereoscopic image. In: High-quality visual experience. Mrak M, Grgic M, Kunt M (eds) Signals and communication technology. Springer, Berlin, Heidelberg, pp 51–77. ISBN: 978-3-642-12801-1. https://doi.org/10.1007/978-3-642-12802-8_3

Chapter 3
Head Tracking for Video Games

Abstract This chapter talks about related work on head gesture recognition and usage of head tracking for several applications including games and virtual reality. An experiment which systematically explores the effects of head tracking, in complex gaming environments typically found in commercial video games is presented. This experiment seeks to find if there are any performance benefits of head tracking in games and how it affects the user experience. We present the results of this experiment along with some guidelines for the game designers who wish to use head tracking for games.

3.1 Introduction

In the previous chapter, we explored potential benefits of stereoscopic 3D in games. We found that stereoscopic 3D provides performance benefits for certain isolated tasks depending on user experience. Just like stereoscopic 3D, head tracking is another technique which could be useful for games. In this chapter we will explore benefits of head tracking in modern video games. Head tracking is commonly used in the virtual and augmented reality communities (Bajura et al. 1992; Marks et al. 2010; Rekimoto 1995) and has potential to be a useful approach for controlling certain gaming tasks. Previous studies (Wang et al. 2006; Yim et al. 2008) have shown that users experience a greater sense of "presence" and satisfaction when head tracking is present. However, these studies were conducted in simple game scenarios. We seek to systematically explore the effects of head tracking, in complex gaming environments typically found in commercial video games, in order to find if there are any performance benefits and how it affects the user experience. A thorough understanding of the possible performance benefits and reasoning behind them would help game developers to make head tracked games not only more enjoyable, but more effective. Our experiment is an initial step towards a foundational understanding of the potential performance benefits of head tracking in modern video games.

© Springer International Publishing AG, part of Springer Nature 2018   33
A. K. Kulshreshth and J. J. LaViola Jr., *Designing Immersive Video Games Using 3DUI Technologies*, Human–Computer Interaction Series, https://doi.org/10.1007/978-3-319-77953-9_3

3.2 Related Work

Head tracking was first reported in the literature in the late 1960's by Sutherland (1968) who attached a mechanical arm to a user's head to detect their head pose. By contrast, modern head-tracking libraries, such as faceAPI (2001); Garage (2000), can now function with just a standard webcam. Following these improvements, researchers have explored the use of head tracking within various desktop applications, including gaming (Bradski 1998; Gorodnichy and Roth 2004). TrackIR (2018) is a commercially available infrared-based head tracking system available which supports several game titles. Another tracking system more recently released, is the Microsoft Kinect. Despite the availability of this hardware, only a few games exist that specifically utilize the head as a gestural controller.

Sko et al. (2009) used head tracking for first-person-shooter (FPS) games and presented a simple two-level taxonomy, which categorized head controlled based techniques into *ambient* or *control*. Ambient (or perceptual) techniques enhance the visual and/or audio feedback based on the user's head position, and control techniques are focused on the controlling the state of the game. Four interaction techniques (zooming, spinning, peering, and iron-sighting) were developed for control and two (head-coupled perspective and handy-cam) for ambient interactions. Their evaluation found that control based techniques are most useful for games which are specifically designed with head tracking in mind and ambient techniques bring more energy and realism in FPS games. However, the main focus of their work was to analyze the effectiveness of each individual technique in isolation and no quantitative measures were involved. In our study we focused on quantitatively measuring the combined affect, on user performance, of simultaneously using several techniques. Yim et al. (2008) developed a low cost head tracking solution based upon the popular work of Johnny Lee (2008) using Nintendo Wii Remotes. Although they did not perform a formal user study, their preliminary results show that users perceived head tracking as a more enjoyable and intuitive gaming experience.

Another experiment (Sko et al. 2013) used webcam-based head tracking in a home setting and collected game data from a large set of users. They used FPS games for their experiment and players reported that the experience was more immersive with head tracking. Based on this experiment, several design guidelines for head tracking usage were proposed. The guidelines include customized setup based on the user's preference, make use of natural head movements, avoid awkward head movements for critical controls, avoid quick head motions and guide the players while playing. Furthermore, their experiments revealed that the participants did not immediately benefit from head tracking usage but they gradually learned and improved their performance with time.

Head gesture recognition techniques based on face tracking, which is similar to head tracking, have been studied by HCI researchers as an input to computer games. Wang et al. (2006) used face tracking for head gesture recognition and developed two basic interaction techniques in two game contexts (avatar appearance & control in a third person game and dodging-and-peeking in a FPS game). Their evaluation, based on simple game prototypes they developed, showed that the test participants experienced a greater sense of presence and satisfaction with their head tracking technique. However, they did not find any differences in user performance compared to using a traditional game controller. Limited accuracy of the head tracking data based on web cam could have been the reason that they did not find any quantifiable performance benefits.

Ashdown et al. (2005) explored head tracking to switch the mouse pointer between monitors in a multi-monitor environment. Although participants preferred using head tracking, their results indicate that the task time was increased with head tracking usage. Another study (Teather and Stuerzlinger 2008) evaluated exaggerated head-coupled camera motions for game-like object movement but did not find any performance differences with different exaggeration levels. Zhu et al. (2009) used head tracking for remote camera control but did not find any benefits of using head tracking compared to keyboard based control. Additionally, they found that users with more gaming experience performed better not only in keyboard controls but also in head tracking controls.

Head tracking has been explored by virtual reality scientists to visualize and understand complex 3D structures (Rekimoto 1995). Bajura et al. (1992) used head tracking for visualizing patient ultrasound data overlapped with a patient image in real time using a head mounted display (HMD). Head tracking has also been used to control avatars in Virtual Environments (VE) (Marks et al. 2010) and it was found that although head tracking is more intuitive for view control, it does not provide any performance benefits compared to using traditional button based controllers.

When using head tracking, the field of view of the display usually limits the head rotations possible if isomorphic mappings are used. If the user rotates his/her head too much then he/she will be looking away from the display (unless head mounted display is used). Several researchers have explored non-isomorphic rotations to get rid of this problem. LaViola et al. (2001) and Jay and Hubbold (2003) both developed non-isomorphic rotation techniques for amplifying head rotations in virtual environments to counteract field of view problems. LaViola et al. developed a technique that gave users a full 360° field of regard in a surround screen virtual environment that had only three walls.

3.3 Our Hypotheses

Based on previous findings in related work and our analysis of the games, we have the following hypotheses:

Hypothesis 1 (H1): Head tracking improves user's gaming performance compared to a traditional game controller.

Hypothesis 2 (H2): Users will learn to play games faster with head tracking on average than with a traditional game controller.

Hypothesis 3 (H3): Users prefer playing games with head tracking since it provides a more engaging user experience.

3.4   User Evaluations

We conducted an experiment with four PC games where participants played each game either with head tracking or without head tracking using the Xbox 360 controller. We examined both quantitative metrics, based on each game's goals and tasks, and qualitative metrics, based on whether participants preferred playing the games with head tracking and whether they perceived any benefits.

3.4.1   Selecting the Games

We chose the TrackIR 5 by NaturalPoint Inc. as our head tracking device because it is natively supported in many (about 130) commercially available games (a list of commercially supported games is available on the TrackIR website TrackIR 2018). TrackIR 5 is an optical motion tracking game controller which can track head motions up to six degrees of freedom, but not all degrees of freedom are supported in all games, depending on the nature of interaction required for that game. Most of these games fall into three categories, racing, flight simulation, and first person shooter. We rejected the games which used head tracking for minimal tasks not related to the objective of the game. We also rejected some old games which did not support rendering at full 1080p resolution. We chose four games, Arma II, Dirt 2, Microsoft Flight and Wings of Prey, that we thought could benefit when played in head tracked environment (see Fig. 3.1). All these games supported alternate control methods, using joystick or buttons on Xbox 360 controller, when head tracking is not available.

Arma II is a first person shooter (FPS) in which users can rotate their heads to look around in the game environment and move their heads closer to screen, in iron-sight (aim using markers on the gun) mode, to shoot distant enemies. We felt that knowledge of the ambient environment, through the use of natural gestures to look around, might help user to find enemies more easily, and zoom-in by moving closer to the screen would make the game more immersive.

Dirt 2 is a car racing game and supports head tracking only in first person view. In this game, users can rotate their heads to rotate the driver's head in the game to look around through the car windows. We expected that this would help users to see upcoming turns more easily and increase their gaming performance.

Microsoft Flight is a flight simulation game and supports head tracking in cockpit view (first person view) mode. In this game, users can also rotate their heads to look around through the windows of the cockpit. Use of head tracking would make it easier for the user to look around for any stationary objects in the flight path in order to avoid collisions.

Wings of Prey is an air combat game in which users shoot enemies while flying. This game is significantly different from Microsoft Flight because in this game you have to shoot moving targets requiring more head usage to find those targets around

(a) **Arma II**

(b) **Dirt 2**

(c) **Microsoft Flight**

(d) **Wings of Prey**

Fig. 3.1 Screenshots of the games used in head tracking experiment

you. In this game, users can look around through the aircraft windows by rotating their head. The aircraft had windows to the left, right, front and top of the player. Looking around naturally would help users find surrounding enemies in the air more easily and would help them increase their performance.

3.4.2 Participants and Equipment

Forty participants (36 males and 4 females ranging in age from 18 to 30 with a mean age of 20.9) were recruited from a university population. A modified version of Terlecki and Newcombe's Video Game Experience survey (Terlecki and Newcombe 2005) was used as a pre-questionnaire in which they answered questions about their previous gaming experience. The survey was modified to include questions related to previous experience, if any, with head tracking, and the games used for the study. Of the 40 participants, 6 were ranked as beginners (4 in head tracked group and 2 in non-head tracked group), 16 as intermediate (7 in head tracked group and 9 in non-head tracked group), and 18 as advanced (9 in each group). Since there were only a few beginners, we decided to combine beginners and intermediate categories into one

Fig. 3.2 The experimental setup for head tracking experiment

category called casual gamers. The experiment duration ranged from 60 to 80 min depending on how long participants took to complete the tasks presented to them in the games and how much time was spent on the questionnaires. All participants were paid $10 for their time.

The head tracked setup (see Fig. 3.2) used a TrackIR 5 with Pro Clip, a Samsung 50" DLP 3D HDTV, a Xbox 360 controller, and a PC (Core i7 920 CPU, GTX 470 graphics card, 16 GB RAM). These are all commodity hardware components.. For the control group, the TrackIR 5 was not used and the participant played only using the Xbox 360 controller. Note that a limitation with head tracking based game camera control is that the maximum amount of head rotation is dependent on the display screen size and distance of user from screen. Too much head rotation could lead you to look away from the screen. This is the reasoning behind our use of a large screen TV for our experiments so, even if users (sitting approximately 3 feets away from the TV screen) rotate their head slightly (about 45° in either direction), they would still be looking at the screen.

3.4.3 Experimental Task

The participants were given the task of playing through levels of the four games. For each game, they were presented with a task specific to that game and a goal for completing each task. Participants played these games in random order (counterbalanced Latin Squares design) with three attempts for each game.

Arma II: Participants played "Single player scenario: Trial by Fire" and their task was to shoot as many enemies as possible within 10 min. The trial ends before 10 min if the player gets shot by the enemy. The game was reset after each trial.

Dirt 2: The participants played "London Rally" and their task was to win the race in as little time as possible with a maximum of 10 min. The game was reset after each trial.

Microsoft Flight: Participants played "First Flight" and their task was to maneuver the aircraft through numerous stationary balloons and finally land on the runway. The aircraft crashes if hit by balloon or if the orientation/speed of aircraft is not right while landing. The game was reset after each trial.

Wings of Prey: The participants played single player mission "Battle of Britain: Defend Manston" and their task was to shoot down all the enemy planes before time runs out (about 5 min). The game ends before the time limit if the aircraft crashes or gets shot down during air combat. After each trial, the game was reset.

3.4.4 Design and Procedure

Our study design was based, in part, on the study by Kulshreshth et al. (2012). We chose a between subjects design to avoid any effects of learning on user performance, where the independent variable was head tracking (with or without) and the dependent variables were the various scoring metrics used in each game. We wanted some additional information about the use of head tracking in video games for those who played the games without head tracking. Thus, we chose to have those participants who played without head tracking, pick one game to try with head tracking in order to gather their reactions. Both the quantitative and qualitative data was explored collectively as well as according to the two player expertise groupings (casuals and experts).

3.4.4.1 Quantitative and Qualitative Metrics

For each game, we tracked quantitative data that we felt was a good indication of how well users performed. Quantitative metrics are summarized in Table 3.1.

In Arma II, survival time and number of enemies shot were tracked as performance metrics. In Dirt 2, we recorded race completion time and rank in the race. In Microsoft Flight, we recorded the game score. The player was scored on the basis of how many balloons it passed through, if proper speed was maintained while landing, and if the plane landed on runway. In case of a plane crash, this game does not show the final score, but does show the points the player gets for each task while playing. We used this to calculate the final score. In Wings of Prey, number of enemies shot, time taken and game score were tracked as performance metrics.

Table 3.1 Summary of metrics for each game used in head tracking experiment. The metrics are used to quantify how users in the head tracked (H) and non-head tracked (NH) groups performed

Game	Metric
Arma II	Number of enemies shot, Survival time
Dirt2	Race completion time, Rank in the race
Microsoft flight	Game score
Wings of prey	Time taken, Number of enemy planes shot

Table 3.2 Post-game questionnaire for head tracking experiment. Participants answered these questions on a 7 point likert scale after playing each game. We used this data for qualitative analysis

Postgame questions	
Q1	To what extent did the game hold your attention?
Q2	How much effort did you put into playing the game?
Q3	Did you feel you were trying your best?
Q4	To what extent did you lose track of time?
Q5	Did you feel the urge to see what was happening around you?
Q6	To what extent you enjoyed playing the game, rather than something you were just doing?
Q7	To what extent did you find the game challenging?
Q8	How well do you think you performed in the game?
Q9	To what extent did you feel emotionally attached to the game?
Q10	To what extent did you enjoy the graphics and the imagery?
Q11	How much would you say you enjoyed playing the game?
Q12	Would you like to play the game again?

Table 3.3 Head tracking questionnaire. Participants responded to statements 1–4 on a 7 point likert scale. Questions 5–10 were multiple choice and open ended questions to gauge the users perception of the effects of head tracking

Head tracking questions	
Q1	Head tracking improved the overall experience of the game.
Q2	I would choose to play head tracked games over normal games.
Q3	I felt that head tracking enhanced the sense of engagement I felt.
Q4	Head tracking is a necessity for my future game experiences.
Q5	Did head tracking help you perform better in the games?
Q6	Which games did it help you in?
Q7	How did it help you in those games?
Q8	Did head tracking decrease your performance in the games?
Q9	Which games did it decrease your performance in?
Q10	How did it decrease your performance in those games?

For the qualitative data, all participants filled out an immersion questionnaire (Jennett et al. 2008) (see Table 3.2) upon completion of all trials of each game. Responses were measured on a 7 point Likert scale (1 = most negative response, 7 = most positive response). Upon completion of all experimental tasks, participants were given a survey to determine how head tracking affected their gaming experience (see Table 3.3), whether they preferred to play the games with head tracking, and if head tracking helped or hurt their performance.

3.4.4.2 Procedure

The experiment began with the participant seated in front of the TV and the moderator seated to the side. Participants were given a standard consent form that explained the study. They were then given a pre-questionnaire that focused on their gaming expertise. Participants were then presented with the games in random order (Latin Squares design). Half the participants played the games without head tracking (control group) and half played with head tracking (experimental group). The moderator would present the game and give instructions to the participant as to what they needed to accomplish in the game and what their goals were. They were also instructed on how to use the Xbox 360 controller. During the experiment, the moderator recorded quantitative data using scores from the games and a stopwatch for timing information (if not already provided by the game). After each game, the participant filled out a post-questionnaire with questions about their experiences with the game. If the participants played the four games in the non-head-tracked condition, they then selected one game to play with head tracking. All participants were given a final post-questionnaire about their experiences with head tracking.

3.5 Results and Analysis

We broke up the participants in each group (head tracked and non-head tracked group) into casual gamers (11 participants in the head tracked group, 11 participants in the non-head tracked group) and expert gamers (9 participants in the head tracked, 9 participants in the non-head tracked group). To analyze the performance data, a two-way ANOVA was conducted that examined the effect of game-play expertise (EXP), casual or expert, and the head tracking mode (HTM), present (H) or absent (NH), on the average (of the three trials) user performance (see Table 3.1 for metrics used for each game). We did a post-hoc analysis using independent sample t-tests. We used Holm's sequential Bonferroni adjustment to correct for type I errors (Holm 1979) and the Shapiro-Wilk test to make sure our data is parametric. We also wanted to see whether there was learning taking place in the form of game play improvement. We looked at the improvement in the performance measures for each game from the first user run to their last run using a repeated measures ANOVA. Finally we wanted to look at the participant's perception of their performance through the post questionnaires. To analyze this Likert scale data, we used the Mann-Whitney test. For all of our statistical measures, we used $\alpha = 0.05$. In all graphs error bars represents 95% confidence interval.

3.5.1 Arma II

Table 3.4 shows the results of a two-way ANOVA analysis for Arma II. Although this table shows some significance based on head tracking mode (HTM), the post-hoc analysis results were not significant. Experts in the head tracking group (H) survived significantly ($t_{16} = 31.94$, $p < 0.01$) longer than the experts in the non-head tracking group (NH) (see Fig. 3.3). For score improvements, neither casual gamers nor expert gamers showed any significant improvements, from the first trial to the last trial, in terms of number of enemies shot and survival times. For the questionnaire data, people thought that the game was too challenging ($\bar{x} = 6.5, \sigma = 0.88$) and they performed badly ($\bar{x} = 2.4, \sigma = 1.28$) in the game. When broken down based on

Table 3.4 Two-way ANOVA analysis for Arma II. Significant differences based on head tracking mode

Source	Enemies shot	Time
HTM	$F_{1,36} = 4.205$, $p < 0.05$	$F_{1,36} = 5.764$, $p < 0.05$
EXP	$F_{1,36} = 3.577$, $p = 0.067$	$F_{1,36} = 3.812$, $p = 0.59$
HTM $\times$ EXP	$F_{1,36} = 0.3611$, $p = 0.440$	$F_{1,36} = 4.656$, $p < 0.05$

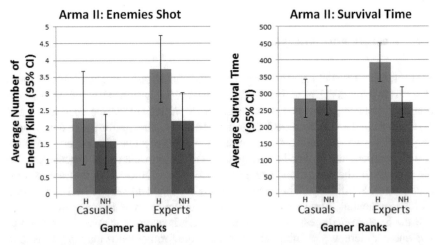

Fig. 3.3 Arma II: Differences in the average number of enemy shot and survival time between the two head tracking modes (H: head tracked, NH: Non-head tracked) in the two gamer categories. Expert gamers performed significantly better with head tracking in terms of survival time

gamer ranks, no significant differences were found on any question in the qualitative data between the two head tracking groups.

3.5.2 Dirt 2

A two-way ANOVA analysis shows (see Table 3.5) significance in the rank based on game expertise. Gamers in the expert group ($\bar{x} = 2.75, \sigma = 1.77$) scored significantly ($t_{38} = 2.794, p < 0.01$) better ranks in the race (lower is better) than the casual gamers ($\bar{x} = 4.16, \sigma = 1.42$) (see Fig. 3.4). For score improvements, casuals in the head tracking group significantly improved their racing time ($F_{2,9} = 5.354, p < 0.05$), from 188.72 s ($\sigma = 81.14$) in the first trial to 152.72 s ($\sigma = 33.72$) in the third trial, and rank ($F_{2,9} = 71.40, p < 0.05$), from 5.36 ($\sigma = 1.50$) in the first trial to 3.81 ($\sigma = 1.83$) in last trial. Casuals in the non-head tracking group significantly improved their racing time as well ($F_{2,9} = 8.449, p < 0.05$), from 171.36 s ($\sigma = 73.87$) in the first trial to 157.36 s ($\sigma = 63.75$) in the third trial, and rank ($F_{2,9} = 4.244, p < 0.05$), from 5.00 ($\sigma = 1.41$) in the first trial to 3.09 ($\sigma = 2.07$) in last trial. This translates to 19.07% improvement for head tracking group compared to 8.16% for non-head

Table 3.5 Two-way ANOVA analysis for Dirt 2. Significant differences in rank based on gaming expertise was found

Source	Race time	Rank
HTM	$F_{1,36} = 0.001, p = 0.980$	$F_{1,36} = 0.003, p = 0.953$
EXP	$F_{1,36} = 3.738, p = 0.061$	$F_{1,36} = 7.467, p < 0.01$
HTM × EXP	$F_{1,36} = 0.090, p = 0.765$	$F_{1,36} = 0.346, p = 0.560$

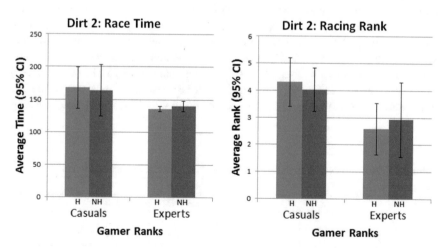

Fig. 3.4 Dirt2: Differences in the average race time and average rank (lower is better) between the two head tracking modes (H: head tracked, NH: Non-head tracked) in the two gamer categories. Expert gamers took less time and scored better rank with head tracking

tracking group in terms of time, and 28.91% improvement for head tracking group compared to 38.20% for non-head tracking group in terms of game rank. Experts in the head tracking group did not show any significance improvements in racing time or rank. Experts in the non-head tracking group significantly improved their racing time ($F_{2,7} = 5.048$, $p < 0.025$), from 146.55 s ($\sigma = 19.04$) in the first trial to 133.22 s ($\sigma = 8.58$) in the third trial, but no significance was found for rank improvement.

For the qualitative data, Dirt 2 held significantly more ($Z = -2.028$, $p < 0.05$) attention for the head tracking group ($\bar{x} = 6.45$, $\sigma = 0.759$) compared to the non-head tracking group ($\bar{x} = 5.7$, $\sigma = 1.380$). All the participants thought they were trying their best ($\bar{x} = 6.10$, $\sigma = 1.277$) to play the game. Casuals in the head tracking group thought that they put in significantly more effort ($Z = -1.96$, $p < 0.05$) to play this game, were significantly less ($Z = -1.997$, $p < 0.05$) distracted, and were trying their best ($Z = -2.144$, $p < 0.05$), compared to the non-head tracked group. Significantly more people ($Z = -1.97$, $p < 0.05$) in the casual head tracking group than in the casual non-head tracked group thought that they would like to play the game again. In the case of expert gamers, the head tracking group enjoyed the graphics and imagery significantly more ($Z = -2.012$, $p < 0.05$) than the non-head tracked group.

3.5.3   Microsoft Flight

No statistically significant differences were found based on head tracking mode or the gamer ranks (see Table 3.6 and Fig. 3.5). Casuals in the head tracking group did not show any significant score improvements, but the casuals in the non-head tracked group significantly improved ($F_{2,9} = 4.865$, $p < 0.05$), their score from 859.09 ($\sigma = 396.11$) in the first trial to 995.45 ($\sigma = 332.00$) in their last trial. In case of experts, the head tracked group significantly improved ($F_{2,9} = 3.811$, $p < 0.05$), their score from 966.66 ($\sigma = 271.569$) in the first trial to the maximum possible score of 1150.0 ($\sigma = 0$) in their last trial, while the non-head tracked group significantly improved ($F_{2,9} = 8.413$, $p < 0.01$), their score from 761.11 ($\sigma = 356.87$) in the first trial to 1122.22 ($\sigma = 66.66$) in their last trial. This translates to 18.97% improvement for head tracking group compared to 47.44% for non-head tracking group.

Table 3.6 Two-way ANOVA analysis for microsoft flight. No significance was found

Source	Game score
HTM	$F_{1,36} = 0.021$, $p = 0.886$
EXP	$F_{1,36} = 2.276$, $p = 0.140$
HTM × EXP	$F_{1,36} = 0.717$, $p = 0.403$

Fig. 3.5 Microsoft Flight: Differences in the game score between the two head tracking modes (H: head tracked, NH: Non-head tracked) in the two gamer categories. Casual gamers performed slightly better without head tracking but expert gamers performed slightly better with head tracking

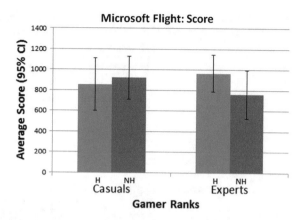

For the qualitative data, the game held the attention of all the participants ($\bar{x} = 5.925, \sigma = 1.047$) and all participants thought that they tried their best ($\bar{x} = 5.975, \sigma = 1.329$). The head tracked group enjoyed the game significantly more ($Z = -2.564, p < 0.05$) and thought that they performed significantly well ($Z = -2.689, p < 0.05$), when compared to non-head tracked group. When broken down based on gamer ranks, no significant differences were found between the two head tracking groups for casual gamers. But, for expert gamers, head tracked group enjoyed the game significantly more ($Z = -2.473, p < 0.05$) than the non-head tracked group.

3.5.4 Wings of Prey

A two-way ANOVA analysis of the Wings of Prey is shown in Table 3.7. The head tracked group ($\bar{x} = 245.56, \sigma = 34.79$) took slightly less ($t_{38} = -2.096, p = 0.043$) time compared to the non-head tracked group ($\bar{x} = 266.45, \sigma = 27.82$) but the results were not significant due to the post-hoc correction. However, experts in the head tracked group ($\bar{x} = 231.51, \sigma = 34.97$) took significantly less ($t_{16} = -2.301, p < 0.05$) time compared to the experts in the non-head tracked group ($\bar{x} = 264.85, \sigma = 25.80$) (see Fig. 3.6). Experts ($\bar{x} = 4.12, \sigma = 2.36$) shot significantly more ($t_{38} = -2.501, p < 0.025$) enemy planes than casual gamers ($\bar{x} = 5.68, \sigma = 1.31$). For score improvement, no significant differences in terms of enemies shot or time taken were found for either casual gamers or expert gamers.

For qualitative data, the game held the attention of all the participants ($\bar{x} = 6.05, \sigma = 1.153$) and all participants thought that they tried their best ($\bar{x} = 6.15, \sigma = 1.291$). Qualitatively, no significant differences were found between the head tracked and non head tracked groups. When broken down based on gamer ranks, there were also no significant differences.

Table 3.7 Two-way ANOVA analysis for wings of prey. Difference in time due to head tracking mode and number of enemies shot due to gaming expertise was found

Source	Enemies shot	Time
HTM	$F_{1,36} = 0.077, p = 0.783$	$F_{1,36} = 5.014, p < 0.05$
EXP	$F_{1,36} = 6.271, p < 0.05$	$F_{1,36} = 2.093, p = 0.157$
HTM × EXP	$F_{1,36} = 2.080, p = 0.158$	$F_{1,36} = 1.325, p = 0.257$

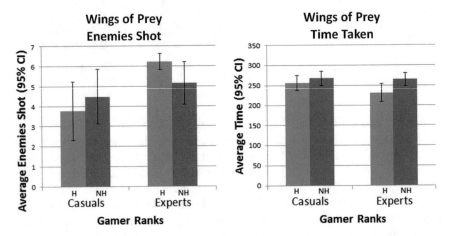

Fig. 3.6 Wings of Prey: Differences in the average number of enemies shot and time taken between the two head tracking modes (H: head tracked, NH: Non-head tracked) in the two gamer categories. Expert gamers shot slightly more enemies and took significantly less time with head tracking

3.5.5 Head Tracking Questions

Out of the 20 participants in the non-head tracked group, three chose to play Arma II, five chose to play Dirt2, three chose to play Microsoft Flight, and nine chose to play Wings of Prey. All three participants who played Arma II thought that head tracking helped them. Only one out of five participants who played Dirt 2 thought that it helped them. Two participants out of three who played Microsoft Flight thought that it helped them. Finally, six out of nine participants who played Wings of Prey thought that it helped them.

Out of the 20 participants from the head tracked group that played all games with head tracking, 19 participants thought that it gave them an advantage in at least one of the games and 13 thought that it hurt their performance in at least one of the games. Eight in Arma II, seven in Dirt 2, and only one in Wings of Prey thought that head tracking hurt their performance. No one thought that head tracking hurt their performance in Microsoft Flight.

All the participants filled out a questionnaire about their experience with head tracking (see Table 3.3), responding to questions Q1–Q4 on a 7 point Likert scale (1 =

Strongly Disagree, 7 = Strongly Agree). All the participants agreed that head tracking improved their overall gaming experience ($\bar{x} = 5.05, \sigma = 1.83$) and enhanced the sense of engagement they felt ($\bar{x} = 5.30, \sigma = 1.69$). However most participants did not think that head tracking was a necessity for their future gaming experience ($\bar{x} = 3.32, \sigma = 1.93$). We did not find any statistically significant differences when data was divided across gamer ranks or head tracking modes.

3.6 Discussion

Hypothesis testing results for each game are summarized in Table 3.8. Hypothesis H1 is true only for expert gamers in case of Arma II and Wings of Prey. Hypothesis H2 was always found to be false which means that head tracking did not help in learning the games faster. Hypothesis H3 was true for casual gamers in Dirt 2 and expert gamers in Microsoft Flight. We noticed large variability, as indicated by large error bars in charts, in our user performance data which could be due to few factors. One factor may be different gaming abilities of the users, an expert FPS gamer may not necessarily be an expert in flight simulation or racing games. Another factor could be insufficient game training time before the experiment.

Based on our quantitative data, we can see that head tracking provided significant performance advantages only for expert gamers for Arma II (better survival time) and Wings of Prey (better time and more number of enemies shot). No other significant advantages were found in the other games we tested. Both Arma II & Wings of Prey are shooting games and in both games head tracking is useful to find enemies around the player's current position. In Arma II, gamers found it useful and natural to rotate their head to look around and move closer to the screen to zoom-in and iron-sight. In the case of Dirt 2, the user had to look forward most of the time and rotating one's head makes it difficult to focus on the road, especially at fast speeds. So, head tracking turned out to be not that useful for this game. In the case of Microsoft Flight, although the head tracking added depth perception and a sense of realism to the game, the game itself was slow paced and not difficult to play. So, users did equally well and it did not matter much if head tracking was present or not.

Table 3.8 Summary of hypothesis (see Sect. 3.4) testing results for all games in the two gamer ranks (T = True and F = False)

Game	Casual gamers			Experts gamers		
	H1	H2	H3	H1	H2	H3
Arma II	F	F	F	T	F	F
Dirt 2	F	F	T	F	F	F
Microsoft flight	F	F	F	F	F	T
Wings of prey	F	F	F	T	F	F

While examining learning effects (e.g., score improvement with each game trial), we noticed that there were significant improvements in some cases when the two groups (head tracked versus non-head tracked) were analyzed separately. However, head tracking usage did not enhance learning, when compared to non-head tracked environment, and in some cases negatively affected learning (e.g., experts in Dirt 2 learned faster without head tracking). But, experts in the head tracking group for Dirt 2 already started with a high score and did not improve much. In the case of Microsoft Flight, the casual non-head tracked group and both expert groups (head tracked vs non-head tracked) improved their score significantly. For Arma II and Wings of Prey, we did not notice any significant improvements across runs. In the case of Arma II, the head tracked group already started with a higher score than the non-head tracked group and did not improve significantly with trials. In the case of Wings of Prey, casual gamers in the head tracked group started with a lower score than the non-head tracked group and both groups did not improve much with repeated attempts. However, expert gamers had a higher score in the head tracked group than the non-head tracked group but it did not improve much with repeated attempts.

Another important factor that could affect our results is the fact that head tracking was an added feature in all the games we tested. So it was up to the user whether to take advantage of head tracking or not. While expert gamers could make better use of head tracking, casual gamers appeared to focus more on games basics and did not pay much attention to head tracking. This may explain why casual gamers performed almost equally well in both the groups (head tracked vs non-head tracked). So far head tracking devices are not as successful as motion controllers (e.g., Sony Move or Nintendo Wii). Games which make use of motion controllers usually provide in-game usage instruction (e.g. a tutorial when the game starts or hints while playing) for their effective use but we found this missing in case of head tracked games we tested. Some instructions could have helped users make better use of head tracking while playing.

Based on our qualitative data, in some games we found significant differences in the two user groups (head tracked vs non-head tracked). Head tracking was perceived to be significantly more enjoyable in Microsoft Flight. Casual users had to put significantly more efforts to play Dirt 2 with head tracking. We did not find any significant differences in Arma II and Wings of Prey. In general, almost all participants were not familiar with the games we tested, and the users played for a short period of time (60 to 80 min). This may explain why we did not notice significant differences in qualitative data for most games.

Additionally, our qualitative data indicates that head tracking is perceived to be more enjoyable for slow paced games and could harm user performance when used in fast paced games. Our results contradict previous findings (Marks et al. 2010; Teather and Stuerzlinger 2008; Zhu et al. 2009), which indicate that although intuitive and enjoyable, head tracking does not provide significant performance benefits. The main reason for these differences could be the choice of game tasks we assigned to participants or the head tracking system used for this study. All the games we tested had native head tracking support and currently there is a limited selection of game genres (Racing, Flight Simulator, and First Person Shooter) that support head tracking, so we need to explore more head tracked based interaction techniques to be able to use them in more game genres. This could be achieved by including tasks in the games which can only be achieved by head tracked-based interaction and bonus points could be given for these tasks. This would force users to use head tracking and help them learn new head tracking based interaction techniques. This could be useful, especially, in the initial phases until head tracking becomes a very commonly used gaming accessory. Based on our findings and observations, we have the following recommendations to game designers:

- Make use of head tracking in FPS and air-combat games because these games have tasks that could benefit from head tracking usage.
- Include instructions/hints while playing games to guide gamers to make optimal use of head tracking. Most people are used to playing games with traditional button based controllers, so most of the time they forget to use head tracking. We think, instructions/hints while playing would remind them of the presence of head tracking.
- Limit head tracking usage in racing games. Head tracking usage could be distracting for racing games.

Note that our study did have some limitations. Due to the nature of experiment and time limitations, it was difficult to balance (in terms of gaming abilities) the participants across the two groups (head tracked vs non-head tracked). Although we had same number of expert users in the two groups, the casual head tracked group had more beginners than the casual non-head tracked group. This disproportion could have skewed some of our results. In addition, unlike previous work (Sko and Gardner 2009; Wang et al. 2006; Yim et al. 2008), the games we tested were complex so it may have been difficult for users to use head tracking effectively and learn how to play the games at the same time. This could have had an affect on performance results.

3.7 Conclusion

We have presented a study exploring the effects of head tracking on user performance in head tracking enabled modern video games. We observed that head tracking could provide significant performance advantages for certain games (Arma II and Wings of Prey) depending upon game genres and gaming expertise. Our results indicate that head tracking is useful in shooting games (FPS, air combat etc.) and it is not a good idea to use it in a fast paced racing games. However, not all users benefit equally well with head tracking. Casual gamers do not benefit significantly from head tracking, but expert gamers can perform significantly better when head tracking is present. A possible reason is that casual gamers focus more on the basic games mechanics and do not pay much attention to a more advanced feature like head tracking. Our qualitative results indicate that head tracking is more enjoyable for slow paced video games (e.g. flight simulation games) and it might hurt performance in fast paced modern video games (e.g. racing games). Our study is a preliminary step towards exploring the effectiveness of head tracking in realistic game scenarios. Clearly, further research with more game genres and head tracking techniques is required to further validate our results.

Now that we understand the potential benefits of stereoscopic 3D and head tracking in games. Next, we need to design menus which are faster and efficient for game tasks. People often use fingers to count or enumerate a list of items so a finger-count based menu could be a better choice to select items on screen, provided we can develop a menu system which is fast enough. In the next chapter, we will explore finger-based menu selection techniques and compare finger-count based menu system with other finger-based techniques in order to determine the best technique.

References

Ashdown M, Oka K, Sato Y (2005) Combining head tracking and mouse input for a GUI on multiple monitors. In: CHI '05 Extended Ab56 stracts on human factors in computing systems. CHI EA '05. ACM, Portland, OR, USA, pp 1188–1191. https://doi.org/10.1145/1056808.1056873 ISBN: 1-59593-002-7

Bajura M, Fuchs H, Ohbuchi R (1992) Merging virtual objects with the real world: seeing ultrasound imagery within the patient. In: SIGGRAPH computer graphics, vol 26, Issue 2, pp 203–210. https://doi.org/10.1145/142920.134061 ISSN: 0097-8930

Bradski GR (1998) Computer vision face tracking for use in a perceptual user interface

Caroline J, Hubbold R (2003) Amplifying head movements with headmounted displays. Presence Teleoperators Virtual Environ 12(3):268–276

Gorodnichy DO, Roth G (2004) Nouse 'use your nose as a mouse' perceptual vision technology for hands-free games and interfaces. In: Image and vision computing, vol 22, Issue 12. Proceedings from the 15th international conference on vision interface, pp. 931–942. http://www.sciencedirect.com/science/article/pii/S0262885604000691, https://doi.org/10.1016/j.imavis.2004.03.021 ISSN: 0262-8856

Holm S (1979) A simple sequentially rejective multiple test procedure. Scand J Stat 6(2):65–70

Jennett C et al (2008) Measuring and defining the experience of immersion in games. Int J Hum Comput Stud 66(9):641–661

Joseph J, LaViola Jr. et al (2001) Hands-free multi-scale navigation in virtual environments. In: Proceedings of the 2001 symposium on interactive 3d graphics. I3D '01. ACM, New York, NY, USA, pp 9–15. https://doi.org/10.1145/364338.364339 ISBN: 1-58113-292-1

Kulshreshth A, Schild J, LaViola JJ Jr (2012) Evaluating user performance in 3D stereo and motion enabled video games. In: Proceedings of the international conference on the foundations of digital games. ACM, New York, NY, pp 33–40. https://doi.org/10.1145/2282338.2282350

Lee J (2008) Hacking the nintendo Wii remote. J IEEE Pervasive Comput 7(3):39–45

Marks S, Windsor JA, Wunsche B (2010) Evaluation of the effectiveness of head tracking for view and avatar control in virtual environments. In: 2010 25th International conference of image and vision computing New Zealand (IVCNZ) pp 1–8. https://doi.org/10.1109/IVCNZ.2010.6148801

NaturalPoint. TrackIR 5 (2018). http://www.naturalpoint.com/trackir/products/trackir5/

Rekimoto J (1995) A vision-based head tracker for fish tank virtual reality-VR without head gear. In: Proceedings of the virtual reality annual international symposium, pp 94–100. https://doi.org/10.1109/VRAIS.1995.512484

Seeing machines. faceAPI (2001). http://www.faceapi.com

Sko T, Gardner H (2009) Head tracking in first-person games: interaction using a web-camera. In: Human-computer interaction - INTERACT 2009, vol 5726. Lecture notes in computer science. Springer, Berlin, pp 342–355. https://doi.org/10.1007/978-3-642-03655-2_38 ISBN: 978-3-642-03654-5

Sko T, Gardner H, Martin M (2013) Studying a head tracking technique for first-person-shooter games in a home setting. In: English. Human-computer interaction INTERACT 2013, vol 8120. Lecture notes in computer science. Springer, Berlin, pp 246–263. https://doi.org/10.1007/978-3-642-40498-6_18 ISBN: 978-3-642-40497-9

Sutherland IE (1968) A head-mounted three dimensional display. In: Proceedings of the fall joint computer conference Part I. December 9–11, 1968, AFIPS '68 (Fall, part I). ACM, San Francisco, California, pp 757–764. https://doi.org/10.1145/1476589.1476686

Teather RJ, Stuerzlinger W (2008) Exaggerated head motions for game viewpoint control. In: Proceedings of the 2008 conference on future play: research, play, share. Future Play '08. ACM, Toronto, Ontario, Canada, pp 240–243. https://doi.org/10.1145/1496984.1497034 ISBN: 978-1-60558-218-4

Terlecki MS, Newcombe NS (2005) How important is the digital divide? The relation of computer and videogame usage gender differences in mental rotation ability. Sex Roles 53:433–441

Wang S et al (2006) Face-tracking as an augmented input in video games: enhancing presence, role-playing and control. In: Proceedings of the SIGCHI conference on human factors in computing systems. CHI '06.Montréal, ACM, Qucébec, Canada, pp 1097–1106. https://doi.org/10.1145/1124772.1124936 ISBN: 1-59593-372-7

Willow garage. OpenCV (2000). http://opencv.willowgarage.com

Yim J, Qiu E, Nicholas Graham, TC (2008) Experience in the design and development of a game based on head-tracking input. In: Proceedings of the 2008 conference on future play: research, play, share. Future Play '08. ACM, Toronto, Ontario, Canada, pp. 236–239. https://doi.org/10.1145/1496984.1497033 ISBN: 978-1-60558-218-4

Zhu D, Gedeon T, Taylor K (2009) Keyboard before head tracking depresses user success in remote camera control. Human-computer interaction, INTERACT 2009, vol 5727. Lecture notes in computer science. Springer, Berlin, pp 319–331. https://doi.org/10.1007/978-3-642-03658-3_37 ISBN: 978-3-642-03657-6

Chapter 4
Gestural Menus for Games

Abstract Menu techniques plays an important role in video games. Since response time and ease of use of a menu system can significantly affect user experience in applications such as video games, it is essential that they be fast, efficient, and not be a burden on the user while setting up and during play. This chapter presents work related to several gesture based menu systems available in literature. We also present a study which seeks to determine the usefulness of finger-count based menu system. Finger-count menus selects an item on screen based on the number of fingers extended by the user. The experiment compares finger-count based menus with several other menus including the 3D Marking menus.

4.1 Introduction

So far we have explored potential benefits of stereoscopic 3D and head tracking in video games. But games do need a better menu system in order to optimize the overall gaming experience. Menu systems are an integral component of any video game and can significantly impact user experience. Due to the availability of various unobtrusive motion sensing devices (e.g., Microsoft Kinect, Leap Motion, Creative Interactive Gesture Camera), many gesture based menu systems (Bailly et al. 2011, Chertoff et al. 2009, Gerber and Bechmann 2005, Ni et al. 2008) have been explored both in academia and commercially in recent years. However, these menu selection methods are often slow (taking about 3–5 s) to perform and can suffer from accuracy problems making them less desirable compared to traditional keyboard-mouse or button based menu systems. Since response time and ease of use of a menu system can significantly affect user experience in applications (such as video games), it is essential that they be fast, efficient, and not be a burden on the user while setting up and during play.

People often use fingers to count or enumerate a list of items. In the past, such finger-counting strategies have been investigated for interaction with multi-touch surfaces (Bailly et al. 2010) and distant displays (Bailly et al. 2011). However, a gestural input system based on finger count gestures (e.g., holding up two fingers) also holds the potential to be a natural and intuitive approach for menu selection

© Springer International Publishing AG, part of Springer Nature 2018

A. K. Kulshreshth and J. J. LaViola Jr., *Designing Immersive Video Games Using 3DUI Technologies*, Human–Computer Interaction Series, https://doi.org/10.1007/978-3-319-77953-9_4

Fig. 4.1 Finger-based menu
selection

in gesture and motion-based games (see Fig. 4.1). We posit that using one's fingers
for menu selection offers several distinct advantages. First, finger count gestures
are easily understood (assuming appropriate menu design) and are fast to perform.
Second, users do not need to move the cursor to different locations on the screen since
finger count gestures are not dependent on the layout of menu items. Third, since no
cursor movement is needed with finger count menus, possible errors in menu item
selection with motion controlled devices are also minimized.

Based on these suppositions, we explored the utility of finger count gestures in two
user evaluations. First, we compared a finger count based menu selection approach
(Finger-Count menu) against two other gestural menu selection techniques (Hand-n-
Hold and Thumbs-Up menu) adapted from existing motion controlled video games.
We examined both menu depth and different menu layouts. Second, we compared the
Finger-Count menu with 3D marking menus (adapted from Marking menus proposed
by Zhao et al. (2004)). In this evaluation, both menu selection strategies also had
an expert selection mode (where users can select menu items without the menu
appearing on screen). In both experiments, we examined selection time, accuracy,
and user preference.

4.2 Related Work

Vision-based hand and finger recognition algorithms have been explored by many
researchers. The Kinect is a popular choice as input device for some of these algorithms (Kulshreshth et al. 2013, Ren et al. 2011, Ryan 2012). Jennings et al. (1999)
used multiple cameras for finger tracking. Kölsch et al. (2004) proposed a robust
hand detection algorithm based on a single camera but their technique requires a
classifier to be trained prior to gesture recognition. Trigo et al. (2010) proposed
an algorithm for detecting finger tips based on template matching. All these techniques are mostly focused on algorithm design and not on investigating interesting
interaction mechanisms based on finger gestures.

Marking menus proposed by Kurtenbach (1993) are gesture based menus where the menu items are arranged in a circle and selection is performed by drawing a mark from the center of the menu towards the desired item. Marking menus support two modes: novice and expert. In novice mode, the user selects a menu item from a circular menu displayed on a screen. In expert mode, the menu is not displayed, forcing a user to trace a continuous sequence of marks from memory, which is then recognized by the system. FlowMenus by Guimbretiére and Winograd (2000) are also based on the Marking menu. FlowMenus let users make a sequence of selections without moving the pen away from the touch surface but no user evaluations were done as part of this work. Zhao et al. (2004) proposed multi-stroke Marking menus with improved accuracy where a user performs a sequence of simple marks instead of a single complex trail. Recently, Marking menus have also been adapted for menu selection in 3D gestural environments (Ren and O'Neill 2012).

Researchers have also explored selection performance of several layouts for menu items on screen. Callahan et al. (1988) showed that menu items in a circular layout can reduce selection time compared to a linear layout in a 2D plane. A similar result was obtained by Komerska and Ware (2004) for their haptic menu system designed for Fishtank VR. Chertoff et al. (2009) designed a Nintendo Wiimote based menu system and found pie menus to be faster than linear lists. The results of all these studies are in line with Fitts's law (Fitts 1954), as pie layouts provide a smaller average distance to menu items.

Several menu techniques have been proposed for virtual environments. TULIP (Bowman and Wingrave 2001) menus assign a menu item to each finger of a pinch glove and selection is made by pinching a finger with the thumb (see Fig. 4.2). Ni et al. (2008) developed the rapMenu (see Fig. 4.3) which is based on hand gestures and requires a pinch glove. To select an item using the rapMenu, the user rotates his wrist to highlight a group of four menu items and then a finger is pinched with the thumb. Spin menus (Gerber and Bechmann 2005) arrange items on a portion of a circle and enabled selection by rotating the wrist in a horizontal plane. Their system

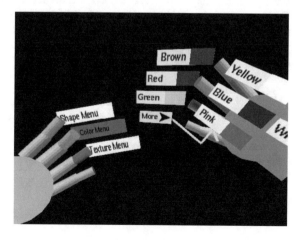

Fig. 4.2 TULIP menus (Bowman and Wingrave 2001)

Fig. 4.3 An illustration of the visual arrangement of the menu items in the 12-item rapMenu (Ni et al. 2008). The four pinch gestures (from index to pinky finger) select 1–4, 5–8, and 9–12 in respective groups. An item is selected by a pinch click,complemented with visual feedback

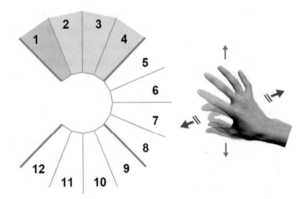

used a workbench from BARCO and an Intersense IS900 Tracker with a wand as an interaction device. Ring menus (Liang and Green 1994) also arrange items in a circle and attached a tracking device to the user's hand. To select an item, users would rotate their hand and move the desired item into a selection bucket. Body centered menus (Mine et al. 1997) assign menu items to parts of a user's body (head not included). These menus do not support hierarchical menu items and due to limited mapping locations on body, the number of menu items is also limited.

4.3   Menu Selection Techniques

This section describes the Hand-n-Hold menu, Thumbs-Up menu, Finger-Count menu, and 3D Marking menu. All these techniques were implemented using a finger/hand recognition algorithm adapted from the fingertip/hand detection algorithm included in the Intel's Perceptual Computing SDK (2018). The main properties of these menu techniques are summarized in Table 4.1. The Creative Interactive Gesture Camera operates at an input frequency of 30 frames per second. We delineate the beginning and end of a selection event by utilizing a frame window of 15 frames to help with segmentation. Thus, each technique requires the user to maintain the selection pose for 0.5 s.

Table 4.1 Properties of menu techniques

	Hand-n-Hold	Thumbs-Up	Finger-Count	3D marking
Gestures	Static	Dynamic	Static	Dynamic
Cursor movement required?	Yes	Yes	No	Yes
Expert mode supported?	No	No	Yes	Yes
Selection time dependent on Layout?	Yes	Yes	No	Yes

Fig. 4.4 Hand-n-Hold menu with vertical layout

4.3.1 Hand-n-Hold Menu

In this technique, users control a cursor by moving their hand in the air (see Fig. 4.4). The position of the cursor on screen is directly related to the 2D position of their hand in a virtual plane. A menu item is selected by holding the cursor over the desired item for a short duration (about one second). If the menu item has a sub-menu then the sub-menu appears in place (replacing the current menu items). The sub-menu items are selected in the same manner as the main menu. This technique requires visual feedback and supports any layout (horizontal, vertical, and circular were implemented) of items. As a pointer based technique, the efficiency of this menu technique is dependent in part on how the items are arranged on screen.

4.3.2 Thumbs-Up Menu

A user holds her fist in front of the input device (see Fig. 4.5). The user then has to move her fist either horizontally, vertically or radially in a virtual plane, depending on the layout, to highlight an item corresponding to their fist position and then give a thumbs up gesture to confirm the selection. Sub-menus appear in place and the selection strategy is the same for sub-menus. Visual feedback is also required for this technique. We chose to use the fist for pointing at menu items because it is extremely easy to transition into the Thumbs-Up gesture from the pointing stance. This technique is similar to Hand-n-Hold in that both require the user to point to an item and then confirm the selection. Hand-n-Hold implements an implicit confirmation mechanism based on a timeout while Thumbs-Up requires explicit

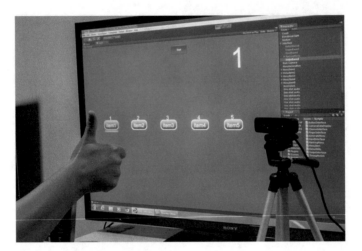

Fig. 4.5 Thumbs-Up menu with horizontal layout

confirmation from a user. Like Hand-n-Hold, this technique is layout dependent, and consequently, its efficiency also depends in part on the spatial arrangement of menu items. It is important to note that while we chose to use a fist for pointing at menu items, theoretically, any hand posture can be used for this purpose, followed by any other gesture for confirmation.

4.3.3 Finger-Count Menu

All the menu items are numbered and the user has to extend a corresponding number of fingers to select a given item (see Fig. 4.6). Items can be arranged in any layout and sub-menus appear in place. We tested three different layouts: horizontal, vertical and circular for this technique. Eyes-free selection is supported since visual feedback is not needed as long as the user knows the corresponding number of the desired item. In novice mode, the menu appears on screen with a number displayed next to each item and the user has to extend a corresponding number of fingers to select an item. In expert mode, the menu does not appear but the selection strategy is the same as novice mode. Expert mode supports a series of finger gestures (extending the appropriate number of fingers) to get to an item under a sub-menu.

This techniques supports using both hands simultaneously, so we can have up to 10 items on screen at a time. In case there are more items, we can label the last item as "Next" indicating that there are more items. If the user selects "Next" then more items appear on screen in place of the original menu. We can extend this idea to include any number of items. Similarly, the last item under a sub-menu can be labeled as "Back." The user can select "Back" to reduce the menu depth and see the parent menu in place.

Fig. 4.6 Finger-Count menu with circular layout

4.3.4 3D Marking Menu

Our 3D Marking menu design is based on the multistroke Marking menu (Zhao and Balakrishnan 2004) because of its higher selection accuracy. The 3D Marking menu gestures are easy to learn and menu item locations can be remembered easily due to spatial memory Bailly et al. (2010). In this technique, the user performs a series of simple gestures instead of a compound stroke. Menu items are always presented to the user in a circular layout. To select an item, the user positions her fist in the center of the menu and moves it towards the desired item, followed by a thumbs up gesture to finalize the selection. Sub-menus appear in place and the selection strategy is the same as the main menu. In novice mode, the menu appears on screen and a single selection is made at a time. In expert mode, the menu is not shown and the user has to perform the required gestures to select an item from memory.

4.4 User Evaluations

We conducted two experiments to evaluate the usefulness of Finger-Count menus. Our first experiment focused on comparing Finger-Count menus with Hand-n-Hold and Thumbs-Up menu selection techniques. We also conducted a second experiment to compare Finger-Count menus with 3D Marking menus. We chose to conduct two experiments because 3D Marking menus support only circular layouts and were very different from Hand-n-Hold and Thumbs-Up. In our pilot tests with two participants, we found the Finger-Count menu to be the fastest technique, therefore we chose to compare only Finger-Count menus with 3D Marking menus. We chose a within-subjects design for our experiments in order to be able to measure and compare user perceptions of the menu selection techniques on a variety of quantitative and qualitative metrics. All menu items were labeled with numbers in our experiments. The setup and participants were the same for both experiments. Participants completed both experiments in order (experiment 1 followed by experiment 2) in a single session. We had the following hypotheses about the chosen menu selection techniques:

Hypothesis 1 (H1): Finger-Count menus are faster than the other menu techniques.
Hypothesis 2 (H2): Finger-Count menus have higher selection accuracy than the other menu techniques.
Hypothesis 3 (H3): People will prefer to use Finger-Count Menus than the other techniques.

4.4.1 Subjects and Apparatus

We recruited 36 participants (31 males and 5 females ranging in age from 18–33) from the University of Central Florida, of which two were left handed. The experiment duration ranged from 50–70 min and all participants were paid $10 for their time.

The experiment setup, shown in Fig. 4.7, consisted of a 55" Sony HDTV and the Creative Interactive Gesture Camera (a readily available and affordable depth sensing camera) mounted on a mini tripod. We used the Unity3D game engine (Unity3D 2013) and Intel Perceptual Computing Software Development Kit (PCSDK) (Intel Perceptual Computing SDK 2018) for implementing all four menu techniques. Participants were seated about 3 feet away from the display and the camera was placed about 1.5 feet away from the participant, in order to ensure that the participant's hand was completely visible to the camera. The position of the camera was changed either to the left or right of the participant, while maintaining the distance from the par-

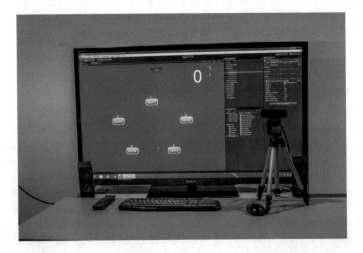

Fig. 4.7 The experimental setup for finger count based menu selection experiment

ticipant, based on dexterity (left handed or right handed) in order to enable optimal viewing of the menu items on screen.

4.4.2 Procedure

The experiment began with the participant seated in front of the TV and the moderator seated to the side. Participants were given a consent form that explained the experiment procedure. They were then given a pre-questionnaire which collected general information about the participant (age, sex, dexterity, etc.). Participants then completed both experiments in order. At the beginning of each experiment, the moderator explained the selection techniques and allowed the user to practice each technique for as long as necessary. Details of experiment tasks are provided in the respective sub-sections of the experiments.

We recorded selection time and accuracy of all the techniques presented in both experiments. For both experiments, selection time was measured as the time from when a random number appeared on screen to the time the corresponding item was selected. Selection accuracy of a technique was measured as the percentage of correct selections out of total selections made for that technique. After each experiment, the participant filled out a post-questionnaire (see Table 4.2) with questions about their experiences with the techniques they tried.

4.4.3 Experiment 1: Hand-n-Hold, Thumbs-Up, and Finger-Count Menu Comparison

The first experiment compared Hand-n-Hold, Thumbs-Up, and Finger-Count menus. All these techniques support horizontal, vertical and circular layouts. Hand-n-Hold and Thumbs-Up only support single handed interactions. As a result, we chose to

Table 4.2 Post-questionnaire. Participants responded to question 1–8 on a 7 point likert scale. Question 9 was a multiple choice question

Post experiment questions	
Q1	To what extent did you like this menu selection technique?
Q2	How mentally demanding was this technique?
Q3	To what extent your arm was tired when using this technique?
Q4	Did you feel hurried or rushed when using this technique?
Q5	How successfully you were able to choose the items you were asked to select?
Q6	Did you feel that you were trying your best?
Q7	To what extent you felt frustrated using this technique?
Q8	To what extent did you feel that this technique was hard to use?
Q9	Which layout of menu items would you prefer for this technique? Horizontal, vertical, circular or all equally?

use a one handed variation of the Finger-Count menu in order to remove a potential confounding variable. Moreover, Hand-n-Hold menu and Thumbs-Up menu do not support expert mode so we did not have any expert mode as part of this experiment.

4.4.3.1 Experiment Design

This within-subjects experiment had 3 independent variables: technique (Hand-n-Hold, Thumbs-Up, and Finger-Count), layout (horizontal, vertical and circular) and menu depth (0 and 1). In total we had $3 \times 3 \times 2 = 18$ conditions and for each condition the user conducted 10 trials which makes a total of 180 selections per participant as part of this experiment. Our dependent variables were average menu selection time and selection accuracy, where the average is taken over the 10 trials for that condition.

Each condition was presented to the user in random order based on a Latin square design (Fisher 1935). For each condition, users were asked to select 10 randomly generated items displayed on screen one item at a time. After completing the experiment, users filled a post-questionnaire (see Table 4.2) with the same set of questions for each technique and then ranked the techniques based on ease of use, arm fatigue, efficiency, and overall best.

4.4.3.2 Quantitative Results

We used repeated-measures 3-factor ANOVA per dependent variable. We did a post-hoc analysis using pairwise sample t-tests. We used Holm's sequential Bonferroni adjustment to correct for type I errors (Holm 1979) and the Shapiro-Wilk test to make sure the data was parametric.

Mean selection time and selection accuracy for each technique is shown in Fig. 4.8. We found significant differences in mean selection time ($F_{2,34} = 363.657, p < 0.005$) and selection accuracy ($F_{2,34} = 45.758, p < 0.005$) between the menu techniques. The Finger-Count menu was faster than Hand-n-Hold ($t_{35} = -21.505, p < 0.005$) and Hand-n-Hold was faster than Thumbs-Up ($t_{35} = -21.433, p < 0.005$). Hand-n-Hold was more accurate than the Finger-Count menu ($t_{35} = -5.586, p < 0.005$), which in turn was more accurate than Thumbs-Up ($t_{35} = 4.488, p < 0.005$).

The Finger-Count menu was the only technique that uses different gestures (different number of fingers extended) for different numbered items. Therefore, we also analyzed the individual gesture error percentage (see Fig. 4.9) and found an overall error rate of 6.81%, with 51.09% of the errors attributed to the gesture for number 3 (three fingers extended) and 28.46% due to the gesture for number 4 (four finger extended).

Menu depth did not have any significant effect on selection time ($F_{1,35} = 1.340, p = 0.255$). Depth showed significant effect on accuracy ($F_{1,35} = 0.258, p < 0.05$) but post-hoc analysis did not find any significant differences.

We also found that the layout of menu items significantly affects the mean selection time of all techniques ($F_{2,34} = 9.384, p < 0.005$). However, there was no signifi-

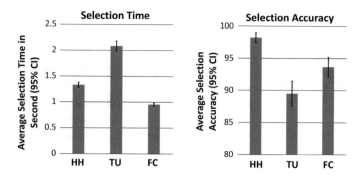

Fig. 4.8 Average selection time and accuracy of each technique where HH is Hand-n-Hold, TU is Thumbs-Up and FC is Finger-Count menu

Fig. 4.9 Error percentage (out of 6.81% errors) of individual gestures for Finger-Count menu. Most of the errors were due gesture 3

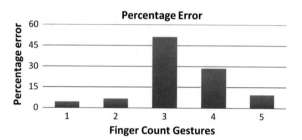

cant effect of item layout on mean selection accuracy ($F_{2,34} = 2.651$, $p = 0.135$). Horizontal layouts were faster than vertical layouts ($t_{35} = -3.095$, $p < 0.005$) and circular layouts ($t_{35} = -4.243$, $p < 0.005$). There was no significant difference in average selection time between vertical layout and circular layout.

We also analyzed each technique separately to study the effects of layout (see Figs. 4.10 and 4.11). The results are as follows:

Hand-n-Hold Menu   Layout had significant effect only on accuracy ($F_{2,34} = 5.548$, $p < 0.05$). A post-hoc analysis revealed that the circular layout was significantly more accurate than the horizontal layout ($t_{35} = -3.366$, $p < 0.005$).

Thumbs-Up Menu   Layout had significant effect on time ($F_{2,34} = 20.563$, $p < 0.005$) and accuracy ($F_{2,34} = 7.776$, $p < 0.005$). The horizontal layout was significantly faster than the vertical ($t_{35} = -4.075$, $p < 0.005$) and the circular layout ($t_{35} = -5.831$, $p < 0.005$). The horizontal layout was significantly more accurate than the vertical layout ($t_{35} = 3.668$, $p < 0.005$).

Finger-Count Menu   As expected, layout had no effect on selection time and accuracy of the Finger-Count menu.

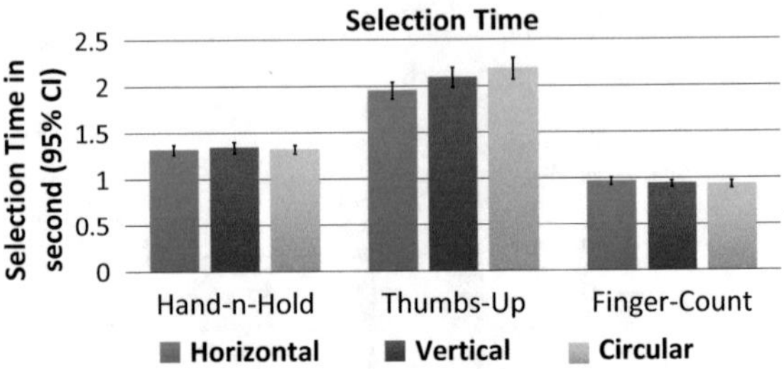

Fig. 4.10 Average selection time of each menu technique for different layouts. The Hand-n-Hold and Finger-Count menus did not have any significant changes in selection time with layout

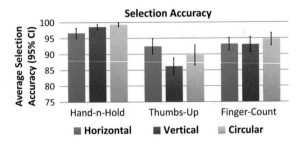

Fig. 4.11 Average accuracy for each layout

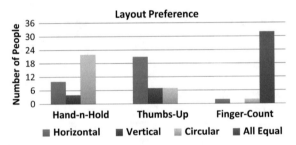

Fig. 4.12 Layout preference for each technique. Finger-Count menus are layout independent

4.4.3.3   Qualitative Results

Based on the post-questionnaire data, 22 people preferred the circular layout for the Hand-n-Hold menu, 21 preferred the horizontal layout for the Thumbs-Up menu, and 32 people thought that all layouts were equivalent for the Finger-Count menu (see Fig. 4.12). The Finger-Count menu was ranked as the overall best technique and the Thumbs-Up menu as the worst technique. The Finger-Count menu was also ranked as best (see Fig. 4.13) in terms of ease of use, efficiency and arm fatigue (less fatigue is better).

To analyze the Likert scale data, we used Friedman's test and then a post-hoc analysis was done using Wilcoxon signed rank tests. These results are displayed in Table 4.3. Median rating for post-questionnaire questions 1–8 is summarized in Fig. 4.14. From the results we an see that:

- People liked Hand-n-Hold and Finger-Count more compared to Thumbs-Up.
- Finger-Count and Hand-n-Hold are mentally less demanding than Thumbs-Up.

Fig. 4.13 Ranking of techniques based on overall best, ease of use, arm fatigue, and efficiency. Finger-Count menu was ranked as the best technique by majority of participants

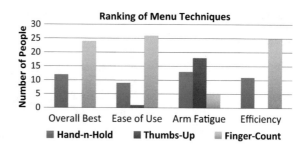

Table 4.3 Results of Friedman's test and post-hoc analysis for Likert scale data of experiment 1. (HH : Hand-n-Hold, TU: Thumbs-Up and FC: Finger-Count)

Question	Friedman's test	HH versus TU	HH versus FC	TU versus FC
Q1	$\chi^2(2) = 41.603$, $p < 0.0005$	$Z = -4.389, p < 0.005$	$Z = -1.649, p = 0.099$	$Z = -4.907, p < 0.005$
Q2	$\chi^2(2) = 19.855$, $p < 0.0005$	$Z = -3.809, p < 0.005$	$Z = -1.029, p = 0.304$	$Z = -3.151, p < 0.005$
Q3	$\chi^2(2) = 35.138$, $p < 0.0005$	$Z = -1.524, p = 0.128$	$Z = -3.780, p < 0.005$	$Z = -4.386, p < 0.005$
Q4	$\chi^2(2) = 17.196$, $p < 0.0005$	$Z = -2.656, p < 0.010$	$Z = -1.837, p = 0.066$	$Z = -3.197, p < 0.005$
Q5	$\chi^2(2) = 35.613$, $p < 0.0005$	$Z = -4.459, p < 0.005$	$Z = -0.996, p = 0.334$	$Z = -3.972, p < 0.005$
Q6	$\chi^2(2) = 3.250$, $p = 0.197$	$Z = -0.000, p = 1.000$	$Z = -1.076, p = 0.282$	$Z = -0.964, p = 0.335$
Q7	$\chi^2(2) = 41.407$, $p < 0.0005$	$Z = -4.778, p < 0.005$	$Z = -0.574, p <= 0.566$	$Z = -4.330, p < 0.005$
Q8	$\chi^2(2) = 41.333$, $p < 0.0005$	$Z = -4.890, p < 0.005$	$Z = -0.330, p = 0.742$	$Z = -4.523, p < 0.005$

- Finger-Count causes less arm fatigue compared to Hand-n-Hold and Thumbs-Up.
- For Thumbs-Up, more people thought they were not able to select items they were asked to select than Hand-n-Hold and Finger-Count.
- Frustration level was higher for Thumbs-Up than Hand-n-Hold and Finger-Count.
- People thought that Thumbs-Up was significantly harder to use than Hand-n-Hold and Finger-Count.

4.4.4 Experiment 2: Compare Finger-Count Menu with 3D Marking Menu

This experiment focused on comparing the Finger-Count menu with a 3D Marking menu. 3D Marking menus support only a circular layout, so we restricted the Finger-

Fig. 4.14 Median ratings for post-questionnaire questions for each technique

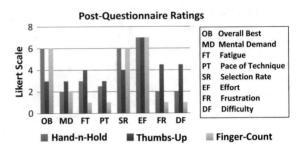

Count menu to a circular layout for a fair comparison. Menu depth for this experiment was set to one in order to the keep the same environment for both novice and expert mode. As 3D Marking menus also only support interaction using a single hand, we again restricted the Finger-Count menu to use a single hand, resulting in a maximum of 5 items per menu.

4.4.4.1   Experimental Design

Our second within-subjects experiment had two independent variables: technique (Finger-Count and 3D Marking menu) and user mode (novice and expert). There were a total of $2 \times 2 = 4$ conditions with 10 trials for each making it a total of 40 selections per participant. Our dependent variables were average menu selection time and average selection accuracy, where the average is taken over 10 trials for that condition. Each condition was presented to the user in a random order based on a Latin square design (Fisher 1935). In novice mode, users were asked to select 10 randomly generated items. In expert mode, a sequence of two numbers were generated for each trial and users were asked to pick the corresponding items in order. After completing the experiment, users filled out a post-questionnaire (only questions 1–8 of Table 4.2) with the same set of questions for each technique.

4.4.4.2   Quantitative Results

A repeated-measures 2-factor ANOVA was used per dependent variable. We did a post-hoc analysis using pairwise sample t-tests. We used Holm's sequential Bonferroni adjustment to correct for type I errors (Holm 1979) and the Shapiro-Wilk test to make sure the data was parametric. Table 4.4 shows the results of repeated measures two-factor ANOVA analysis.

The Finger-Count menu was significantly faster (see Fig. 4.15) than the 3D Marking menu in both novice mode ($t_{35} = 11.868$, $p < 0.0005$) and expert mode ($t_{35} = 10.942$, $p < 0.0005$). In novice mode, the average selection time was 0.933 seconds ($\sigma = 0.098$) for the Finger-Count menu and 2.09 seconds ($\sigma = 0.643$) for the 3D Marking menu. In expert mode, selection time was 2.307 seconds ($\sigma = 0.223$)

Table 4.4 Repeated measure 2-factor ANOVA analysis for comparing the 3D Marking menu with the Finger-Count menu. There was significant difference in selection time based on menu technique as well as mode. Accuracy was significantly different between the user modes

Source	Selection time	Accuracy
Technique	$F_{1,35} = 145.774, p < 0.0005$	$F_{1,35} = 0.864, p = 0.359$
Mode	$F_{1,35} = 751.146, p < 0.0005$	$F_{1,35} = 11.887, p < 0.005$
Technique $\times$ Mode	$F_{1,35} = 26.831, p < 0.0005$	$F_{1,35} = 1.755, p = 0.194$

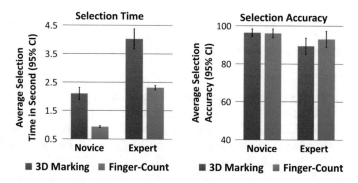

Fig. 4.15 Selection time and accuracy by technique and mode

for the Finger-Count menu and 4.024 seconds ($\sigma = 1.067$) for the 3D Marking menu. Overall, there was no significant difference in selection accuracy between the menu techniques (see Fig. 4.15). Novice mode had significantly higher selection accuracy than expert mode ($t_{35} = 3.448, p < 0.005$). Average selection accuracy was 96.25% ($\sigma = 5.123$) for novice mode and 91.25% ($\sigma = 9.131$) for expert mode.

4.4.4.3 Qualitative Results

The qualitative data was analyzed separately for novice and expert modes. To analyze the Likert scale data, we used Wilcoxon signed rank tests. Median ratings for post-questionnaire questions 1 to 8 are summarized in Fig. 4.16.

In novice mode (see Fig. 4.16), people liked the Finger-Count menu significantly more than the 3D Marking menu ($Z = -4.059, p < 0.0005$). The 3D Marking menu is significantly more mentally demanding than the Finger-Count menu ($Z = -3.272, p < 0.005$). The 3D Marking menu also lead to significantly more arm fatigue than the Finger-Count menu ($Z = -3.383, p < 0.005$). People thought that using the Finger-Count menu let them select items with significantly higher accuracy than the 3D Marking menu ($Z = -3.106, p < 0.005$). People also felt significantly less frustrated with the Finger-Count menu than the 3D Marking menu ($Z = -3.778, p < 0.0005$). Finally, the 3D Marking menu was significantly harder to use than the Finger-Count menu ($Z = -3.357, p < 0.005$).

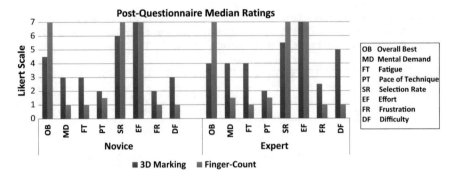

Fig. 4.16 Median ratings for post-questionnaire questions for each technique

Statistics for expert mode were similar to novice mode (see Fig. 4.16). In expert mode, people liked the Finger-Count menu significantly more than the 3D Marking menu ($Z = -4.335$, $p < 0.0005$). The 3D Marking menu is significantly more mentally demanding than the Finger-Count menu ($Z = -4.196$, $p < 0.005$). 3D Marking menu usage also lead to significantly more arm fatigue than the Finger-Count menu ($Z = -4.115$, $p < 0.0005$). People thought that when using Finger-Count menus they were able to select items with significantly higher accuracy than with the 3D Marking menu ($Z = -3.751$, $p < 0.005$). People felt significantly less frustrated with the Finger-Count menu ($Z = -3.348$, $p < 0.005$). Finally, the 3D Marking menu was significantly harder to use than the Finger-Count menu ($Z = -4.307$, $p < 0.0005$).

4.5 Discussion

Our experiments indicate that Finger-Count menus let participants select items significantly faster than either Hand-n-Hold, Thumbs-Up or 3D Marking menus. This is primarily because Finger-Count menus do not require the user to move their hand in accordance with the position of items on screen, resulting in a constant selection time for all items. For Hand-n-Hold menus, the second-fastest technique, the user has to continuously move his hand to select an item, increasing the selection time. Thumbs-Up not only requires a user to move his hand for selecting a menu item, but to also give a thumb's up gesture to finalize the selection. 3D Marking menus have similar hand motion characteristics as Thumbs-Up, as both techniques require hand motion and then an explicit thumbs-up gesture to finalize item selection. This additional motion and a gesture takes significantly more time than simply extending one's fingers.

We found that Hand-n-Hold was the most accurate out of all selection techniques tested because it involves controlling a pointer with one's hand with implicit finalization, making it less error prone than recognizing extended fingers or the thumb's up gesture. Even though Hand-n-Hold is the most accurate technique, we found that users preferred Finger-Count menus more because of its faster selection time and its natural interaction metaphor. In the future, we foresee better selection accuracy for Finger-Count menus due to the availability of better gestural input devices and recognition algorithms.

Our analysis of menu item layout presents an interesting picture. Finger-Count menus have a constant selection time and are not at all affected by the layout of menu items. For Hand-n-Hold, item layout did not have any effect on selection time but circular layouts resulted in higher selection accuracy than horizontal and vertical layouts, probably due to the similar spacing of menu items, resulting in a similar amount of movement. When using Hand-n-Hold with horizontal and vertical layouts, participants occasionally tended to accidentally bump into wrong items while moving the pointer to a desired item, resulting in a wrong selection. But with circular layouts, they could keep the pointer inside the circle and reach all menu items at the periphery without accidentally selecting other items. For Thumbs-Up, we found that horizontal layouts resulted in faster selection and increased selection accuracy. We believe this is primarily because a person's arm has a more natural and relaxed posture when moved horizontally. In the case of vertical and circular layouts, participants often oriented their hand in such a way that their thumb was not pointing upwards making it difficult for the gesture recognizer to identify it as a thumb's up gesture. This orientation decreased the mean selection accuracy in these layouts for Thumbs-Up.

For Finger-Count menus, three fingers can present a possibly difficult combination for detection because users in our experiments tended to keep the middle finger and ring finger close enough to be detected as a single finger. However, detecting the number four proved easier because participants automatically provided sufficient spacing to alleviate confusion in the recognizer. This issue can also be remedied by using both hands simultaneously (e.g., index finger in one hand and index and middle finger in the other hand to indicate a 3 gesture). Our implementation of Finger-Count menus support using both hands simultaneously. But since the other techniques in our study were single handed only, we restricted Finger-Count menus to use single hand interaction for a fair comparison.

Our subjective responses indicate that Finger-Count menus were the most pre-ferred and most efficient, had the least arm fatigue, and was the least frustrating technique. This seems promising for future games and applications with short range gestural input. Participants were impressed by the selection time of the Finger-Count menus. The second most preferred technique was Hand-n-Hold because of its ease of use and high accuracy. People are used to controlling a pointer using a mouse and this technique seems familiar to them. People did not like Thumbs-Up because of high error rate. Participants thought that 3D Marking menus are more mentally demanding than the Finger-Count menu. This is because for Finger-Count menus, the user does not have to worry about the location of items on screen. This fact is much more noticeable in expert mode where the menu does not appear on screen. For 3D Marking menus, people need to memorize the location of items with respect to the center to be able to perform a radial mark to select the desired item. Finger-Count menus were rated as less frustrating and most liked technique than the 3D Marking menu.

Based on the results of our experiments, we were able to accept H1, H3 and were unable to accept H2. Consequently, we believe that Finger-Count menus have the potential to be used as a menu system in future 3D gesture controlled applications and video games. Finger-Count menus have a very low response time making users spend a minimal amount of time interacting with menus. All the Finger-Count gestures are intuitive and easy to remember. Both casual and expert gamers could use this technique with a limited learning curve. Once players get used to the menu system, they can transition to expert mode and can change game setting (e.g., change appearance of game character, selecting a weapon from inventory, switching camera position in racing games, etc.) with no interference from menu items on screen. It could also be a good idea to mix traditional mouse based menus with Finger-Count menus. Mouse pointer menus could be used to select game settings at the beginning of a game and Finger-Count menus for changing in-game settings while playing. For example, in a gesture controlled car racing game, a user can set display resolution, select a track and car using traditional menus. While racing, he can switch between first person view to third person view using Finger-Count menus. Similarly, a user could select weapons from an inventory for a First Person Shooter (FPS) games using Finger-Count menus. Finger-count menus could be combined with other hand gestures to increase the number of possible gestures thereby increasing the number of possible motion controlled tasks in video games.

There are a few factors that could have affected our results. When comparing layouts for a given technique, items were equally spaced for a given layout but the item spacing was not the same across the three layouts. It could have a minor effect on our results but we still believe that horizontal layout would be slightly faster than vertical layout for hand based interaction because a person's arm has more natural and relaxed posture when moved horizontally. The shape of the menu items could also have had some influence on how well users perform in an horizontal or vertical layout. Ideally, a circular menu item would be more balanced across all dimensions but we don't find such menu items in video games. Hence, circular menu items were not considered to simulate real world menu items. Our study design could also have had an influence on our results. The two experiments were performed in order, experiment 1 and then experiment 2 but conditions in each experiment were randomized. This could have some effect on our results but we believe that people would have still preferred Finger-count menus over 3D Marking menus (in experiment 2) due to its ease of use and fast response time. Moreover, we did not consider studying learning effects because all the gestures performed were easy to learn requiring very little time to train the users.

Finger-Count menus do have some limitations. Hand physiology also plays an important role. Some people found it difficult to keep their fingers separated. One of the participants had arthritis in one hand. It was difficult for him to keep enough separation between the fingers to be counted as separate fingers by the recognizer. But the Finger-Count menu worked fine for him when he used his other hand. We think that it could also be a problematic for some old age people because of the weakening of intrinsic hand muscles with age (Shweta 2010). Thus, such an interface could be a challenge for people with arthritis or any form of ailment preventing them from keeping their fingers separated for the gesture recognizer.

4.6 Conclusion

We presented an in-depth exploration comparing Finger-Count menus with Hand-n-Hold, Thumbs-Up, and 3D Marking menus using different layouts and modes (novice and expert). Our results show that Finger-Count menus are a viable option for 3D menu selection tasks with fast response times and high accuracy and could be well suited for gesture controlled applications such as games. In terms of horizontal, vertical and circular layouts, selection time and selection accuracy of Finger-Count menus did not change with layout. However, the circular layout had higher selection accuracy for Hand-n-Hold menus while the horizontal layout was faster and more accurate for Thumbs-Up menus. A significantly higher number of participants ranked Finger-Count menus as their favorite technique and the second best technique was the Hand-n-Hold menu.

In Chap. 2, we explored potential benefits of stereoscopic 3D in games. The games we used in our experiment generate stereoscopic 3D images using fixed stereoscopic parameters (separation and convergence) which may not always be optimal. In the next chapter, we will explore how we can optimize stereoscopic 3D, to enhance depth discrimination in the scene, using dynamic adjustments to the stereoscopic parameters.

References

Bailly G et al (2011) Comparing free hand menu techniques for distant displays using linear, marking and finger-count menus. In: Human-computer interaction INTERACT 2011 LNCS, vol. 6947. Springer, Heidelberg, pp 248–262. https://doi.org/10.1007/978-3-642-23771-3_19 ISBN: 978-3-642-23770-6

Bailly G, Lecolinet E, Guiard Y (2010) Finger-count and radial-stroke shortcuts: 2 techniques for augmenting linear menus on multi-touch surfaces. In: Proceedings of the SIGCHI conference on human factors in computing systems. CHI'10. ACM, New York, pp 591–594. https://doi.org/10.1145/1753326.1753414

Bowman DA, Wingrave CA (2001) Design and evaluation of menu systems for immersive virtual environments. In: Proceedings of the virtual reality. IEEE, pp 149–156. https://doi.org/10.1109/VR.2001.913781

Callahan J et al (1988) An empirical comparison of pie vs. linear menus. In: Proceedings of the SIGCHI conference on human factors in computing systems. CHI '88. ACM, USA, pp 95–100. https://doi.org/10.1145/57167.57182 ISBN: 0-201-14237-6

Chertoff DB, Byers RW, LaViola Jr. JJ (2009) An exploration of menu techniques using a 3D game input device. In: Proceedings of the 4th international conference on foundations of digital games. FDG '09. ACM, Florida, pp 256–262. https://doi.org/10.1145/1536513.1536559 ISBN: 978-1-60558-437-9

Fisher RA (1935) The design of experiments. Oliver and Boyd, England

Fitts PM (1954) The information capacity of the human motor system in controlling the amplitude of movement. J Exp Psychol 47(6):381–391. https://doi.org/10.1037/0096-3445.121.3.262

Gerber D, Bechmann D (2005) The spin menu: a menu system for virtual environments. In: Proceedings of the 2005 IEEE conference 2005 on virtual reality. VR '05. IEEE Computer Society, USA, pp 271–272. https://doi.org/10.1109/VR.2005.81 ISBN: 0-7803-8929-8

Guimbretiére F, Winograd T (2000) FlowMenu: combining command, text, and data entry. In: Proceedings of the 13th annual ACM symposium on User interface software and technology. UIST '00. ACM, USA, pp 213–216. https://doi.org/10.1145/354401.354778 ISBN: 1-58113-212-3

Holm S (1979) A simple sequentially rejective multiple test procedure. Scandinavian J Stat 6(2):65–70

Intel Perceptual Computing SDK (2018). http://software.intel.com/en-us/vcsource/tools/perceptual-computing-sdk.

Jennings C (1999) Robust finger tracking with multiple cameras. In: Proceedings of the international workshop on recognition, analysis, and tracking of faces and gestures in real-time systems, pp 152–160. https://doi.org/10.1109/RATFG.1999.799238

Kölsch M, Turk M (2004) Robust hand detection. In: Proceedings of the sixth IEEE international conference on Automatic face and gesture recognition. IEEE Computer Society, pp 614–619

Komerska R, Ware C (2004) A study of haptic linear and pie menus in a 3D fish tank VR environment. In: Proceedings of the 12th International Symposium on haptic interfaces for virtual environment and teleoperator systems, 2004. HAPTICS '04, pp 224–231. https://doi.org/10.1109/HAPTIC.2004.1287200

Kulshreshth A, Zorn C, LaViola J (2013) Real-time markerless kinect based finger tracking and hand gesture recognition for HCI. In: Proceedings of the IEEE Symposium on 3D user interfaces, pp 187–188

Kurtenbach GP (1993) The design and evaluation of marking menus. Ph.D. thesis. University of Toronto, Canada

Liang J, Green M (1994) JDCAD: A highly interactive 3D modeling. Computers and graphics, vol 18, 4 pp 499–506

Mine MR, Brooks FP, Sequin CH (1997) Moving objects in space: exploiting proprioception in virtual-environment interaction. SIGGRAPH. ACM, pp 19–26

Ren G, O'Neill F (2012) 3D marking menu selection with freehand gestures. In: IEEE symposium on 3D user interfaces. IEEE, pp 61–68

Ren Z, Yuan J, Zhang Z (2011) Robust hand gesture recognition based on finger-earth mover's distance with a commodity depth camera. In: Proceedings of the 19th ACM international conference on multimedia. MM '11. ACM, USA, pp 1093–1096. https://doi.org/10.1145/2072298.2071946 ISBN:978-1-4503-0616-4

Ryan DJ (2012) Finger and gesture recognition with microsoft kinect MA thesis, University of Stavanger, Norway. http://brage.bibsys.no/uis/handle/URN:NBN:no-bibsys_brage_33088

Shweta K, Zatsiorsky VM, Latash ML (2010) Age-related changes in the control of finger force vectors. J Appl Physiol 109(6):1827–1841

Tao N, McMahan RP, Bowman DA (2008) Tech-note: rapMenu: remote menu selection using freehand gestural Input. In: IEEE symposium on 3D user interfaces, pp 55–58

Trigo TR, Pellegrino SRM (2010) An analysis of features for hand-gesture classification. In: 17th international conference on systems, signals and image processing (IWSSIP 2010), pp 412–415

Unity3D (2013). http://unity3d.com/.

Zhao S, Balakrishnan R (2004) Simple versus compound mark hierarchical marking menus. Proceedings of the 17th annual ACM symposium on User interface software and technology. ACM, pp 33–42. https://doi.org/10.1145/1029632.1029639

Chapter 5
Dynamic Stereoscopic 3D Parameters

Abstract Stereoscopic 3D displays present two images offset to the left and right eye of the user and these images are then fused by the brain to give the perception of 3D depth. The generation of these two images uses two stereo parameters: separation and convergence. Currently, most stereoscopic 3D applications fix convergence and separation values for optimal viewing during usage time. However, this approach reduces stereo depth in certain scenarios. This chapter discusses work related to dynamic stereoscopic 3D parameters to generate better 3D images. We present our experiment which aims to improve depth perception using dynamic stereoscopic parameters.

5.1 Introduction

Stereoscopic 3D displays present two images offset to the left and right eye of the user and these images are then fused by the brain to give the perception of 3D depth. The generation of these two images uses two stereo parameters: separation and convergence. Separation is defined as the interaxial distance between the centers of the two virtual eye camera lenses in the scene and the convergence is defined as the distance of the plane where left and right eye camera frustums intersect (see Fig. 5.1). Currently, most stereoscopic 3D applications fix convergence and separation values for optimal viewing during usage time. However, this approach reduces stereo depth in certain scenarios. Two examples are when the depth range has a large variability between different scenes (e.g. transition from inside a room to an outdoor scene) and when a large object (e.g. a gun in FPS games, the cockpit in air-combat games, etc.) is present in front of the camera. The fact that these parameters are optimized to minimize visual discomfort uniformly during usage usually limits the convergence and separation values. Depth discrimination (the ability to judge relative depths of objects in the scene) in a stereo 3D application could potentially be improved if the stereo parameters are dynamically adjusted based on the scene.

© Springer International Publishing AG, part of Springer Nature 2018   73
A. K. Kulshreshth and J. J. LaViola Jr., *Designing Immersive Video Games Using 3DUI Technologies*, Human–Computer Interaction Series, https://doi.org/10.1007/978-3-319-77953-9_5

5.2   Related Work

Stereo comfort could be increased by either changing stereo parameters or using depth of field (DOF) blurring. Ware (1995) proposed dynamic adjustment of stereoscopic parameters to minimize visual discomfort and optimize stereo depth. Furthermore, their results revealed that the separation must be changed gradually over a few seconds to allow users to adjust without noticing any visual distortion of the scene. Bernhard et al. (2014) explored dynamic adjustment of stereo parameters using gaze data and found that it reduces stereo fusion time and provides a more comfortable viewing experience. The past work on dynamic stereo mentioned above used simple static scenes (e.g. random-dot stereograms, a picture, etc.) to evaluate their work. None of the work explored the benefits of dynamic stereo in complex scenes like in modern video games.

Several researchers (Bernhard et al. 2014; Duchowski et al. 2014; Vinnikov and Allison 2014) have explored gaze based depth of field (DOF) effects to minimize visual fatigue. However, people generally disliked the DOF effect with temporal lag of the gaze-contingent effect being a possible reason. Maiello et al. (2014) explored the interaction of stereo disparity parameters and DOF blur on stereo fusion. They found that DOF blur helped the stereo fusion process but only if the blur was present on the visual periphery. Mauderer et al. (2014) used gaze contingent DOF to produce realistic 3D images and found that it increases the sense of realism and depth. But, their system had limited accuracy in terms of depth judgment of the objects in the scene.

The past work on dynamic stereo mentioned above used simple static scenes (e.g. random-dot stereograms, a picture, etc.) to evaluate their work. None of the work explored the benefits of dynamic stereo in complex scenes like in modern video games. To the best of our knowledge, our work is the first to systematically explore dynamic stereo for more complex dynamic scenes.

5.3   Dynamic Stereoscopic 3D

Stereo parameters (separation and convergence) could be optimized based on the type of scene. Ideal application candidates for these optimizations could be classified in two broad categories. The first category is an application where there is a large variation in depth range across scenes and the second category is an application which always has a large object in front of the camera.

5.3.1   Type 1: Large Depth Range Variation

The separation value is dependent on the depth range of the scene. For better depth discrimination, the separation is directly proportional to the maximum depth in the scene. Similarly, the convergence distance is also limited by the depth in the scene for a comfortable viewing experience. When there is a large depth variation across

Fig. 5.1 Off-axis stereo
projection

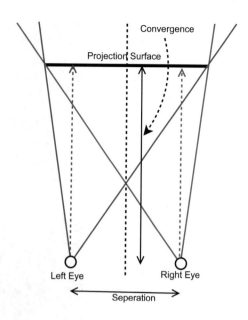

scenes, the separation and convergence values have to be set based on the scene with least depth range. If the separation and the convergence values are set based on a scene with large depth then they will make another scene with less depth uncomfortable to look at. Therefore, these parameters must be changed dynamically from scene to scene for more depth discrimination in all the scenes.

We implemented a scene which has a limited depth in one direction and a large depth range in the opposite direction (see Fig. 5.2). Head tracking is used to control the head of a first person controller (FPC) and a mouse is used to rotate the body of the FPC. The convergence value is dynamically changed based on the object being looked at and the separation is changed based on the depth range of the scene in front of the camera (see Algorithm 5.1 for details). The convergence and the separation values are changed gradually, as proposed by Ware (1995), to allow enough time for the user's eyes to adjust.

5.3.2 Type 2: Large Object in Front of Camera

When a large object (e.g. a gun in FPS games, the cockpit in air-combat, etc.) is present in front of the camera, the stereo parameters have to be optimized to keep that large object always in focus thereby limiting the depth discrimination. However, when the player's head is rotated/translated, that nearby object may not be in the player's view and stereo depth could be increased.

We implemented an air combat game scene (see Fig. 5.3) as a representative of this category of applications. In the game, the player has to control an aircraft, using a joystick, in a first person view controlled using head tracking. In addition, the user

Fig. 5.2 Scene 1: a scene
with variable depth range
across different directions

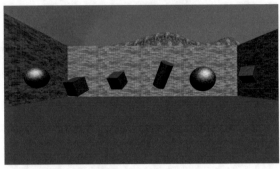

(a) Depth is limited by wall in this direction

(b) Unlimited depth in this direction

can move his/her head closer to the screen to zoom into the scene for iron-sighting
distant enemies. We optimized stereo parameters under two conditions. First, when
the user is looking sideways (left/right) and second, when the user is zoomed into the
scene (see Algorithm 5.2 for details). In both of these cases, the user is not looking at
the cockpit. When the player's head is rotated sideways (left/right), the separation is
increased with linear scaling proportional to the head's rotation and the convergence
is not changed. When a user zooms in the scene, the separation is increased with linear
scaling proportional to the head's displacement. At the same time, the convergence
is linearly decreased with the head's displacement to keep both the crosshair and
background in focus. These dynamic parameters ensured a comfortable stereoscopic
3D experience and provided better depth discrimination for this air-combat game.

5.3.3 Implementation Details

We used Nvidia's 3D vision for our implementation and thus used the NVAPI library
to change the convergence and the separation. According to the NVAPI library, the
normalized eye separation is defined as the ratio of the interocular distance (between
the eyes) and the display screen width. The separation value used in the driver is
a percentage of this normalized eye separation and hence is a value between 1 and

Fig. 5.3 Scene 2: a scene with a large object in front of the camera

100. Convergence is defined as the distance (in meters) of the plane of intersection of the left and right eye camera frustums with off-axis (or parallel) projection (see Fig. 5.1). Projection matrices were calculated automatically by the driver.

Scene 1. For static stereo, the convergence was set to 1.0 and the separation was set to 20.0. In the case of dynamic stereo, the algorithm is described in Algorithm 5.1. We set $SF = 3$, $threshold = 50$, $C_1 = 30$, $S_1 = 20$ and $S_2 = 50$ in the implementation. These values were obtained based on several pilot studies for Scene 1.

Algorithm 5.1 Calculate stereo parameter for scene 1

1: $S_1 \leftarrow$ separation for lower depth range
2: $S_2 \leftarrow$ separation for higher depth range
3: $C_1 \leftarrow$ convergence for higher depth range
4: $SF \leftarrow$ smothing factor
5: $threshold \leftarrow$ depth threshold
6: $\Delta t \leftarrow$ time between frames rendered on screen
7: $t \leftarrow SF \times \Delta t$
8: $C \leftarrow 1.0$
9: $S \leftarrow S_1$
10: Use raycast to find object Obj in front of camera
11: $d \leftarrow$ distance of Obj
12: **if** $d < threshold$ **then**
13:     $C \leftarrow C + (d - C) \times t$
14:     $S \leftarrow S + (S_1 - S) \times t$
15: **else**
16:     $C \leftarrow C + (C_1 - C) \times t.$
17:     $S \leftarrow S + (S_2 - S) \times t.$
18: $convergence \leftarrow C$
19: $separation \leftarrow S$

Scene 2. For static stereo, the convergence was set to 4.0 and the separation was set to 5.0. The dynamic stereo algorithm is described in Algorithm 5.2. We set $C_0 = 4.0, C_1 = 0.001, S_0 = 5.0, S_1 = 60.0, roty_1 = 10$ and $roty_2 = 60.0$ in our implementation. These values were obtained based on several pilot studies for Scene 2.

Algorithm 5.2 Calculate stereo parameter for scene 2

1: $ihp \leftarrow$ initial head position
2: $mhp \leftarrow$ head position when completely zoomed in
3: $chp \leftarrow$ current head position
4: $roty \leftarrow$ current head rotation along y-axis
5: $roty_1 \leftarrow$ min head rotation along y-axis
6: $roty_2 \leftarrow$ max head rotation along y-axis
7: $C_0 \leftarrow$ initial convergence
8: $C_1 \leftarrow$ final convergence after zooming
9: $S_0 \leftarrow$ initial separation
10: $S_1 \leftarrow$ maximum separation
11: $C \leftarrow C_0$
12: $S \leftarrow S_0$
13: \\zoom in case
14: **if** $|ihp - chp| > 0$ **then**
15:     $C \leftarrow C_1 + (C_0 - C_1) \times (mhp - chp)/(mhp - ihp)$
16:     $S \leftarrow S_1 + (S_0 - S_1) \times (mhp - chp)/(mhp - ihp)$
17: \\look left/right case
18: **if** $roty > roty_1$ and $roty < roty_2$ **then**
19:     $C \leftarrow C_0$
20:     $S \leftarrow S_1 + (S_0 - S_1) \times (roty_2 - roty)/(roty_2 - roty_1)$
21: **else if** $roty > roty_2$ **then**
22:     $C \leftarrow C_0$
23:     $S \leftarrow S_1$
24: $convergence \leftarrow C$
25: $separation \leftarrow S$

5.4 User Evaluations

We conducted an experiment to evaluate the effectiveness of dynamic stereo parameters. We recruited 12 participants (10 males and 2 females ranging in age from 18 to 33 with a mean age 27.83) from the university population. The experiment duration ranged from 20 to 30 min. The experiment setup is shown in Fig. 5.4. We used the Unity3D game engine for implementing the scenes. The TrackIR 5 camera and the Nvidia IR emitter were mounted on the top of monitor. Participants were seated about 2 feet away from the display. To make sure that all our participants were able to see stereoscopic 3D, we used the Nvidia medical test image to test stereo abilities of participants and all our participants passed the test. Note that Nvidia 3D glasses

Fig. 5.4 The experiment setup consisted of a 27" BenQ XL2720Z 3D monitor, Nvidia 3D vision kit, a TrackIR 5 with pro clip (mounted on a headphone), a logitech extreme 3D pro joystick, and a PC (Core i7 4770K CPU, GTX 780 graphics card, 8 GB RAM)

Table 5.1 Post-questionnaire. Participants responded to question 1–3 on a 7 point Likert scale. In question 4, each symptom had a 7 point Likert scale to indicate the extent of each symptom ranging from not at all to very much so

Questionnaire	
Q1	To what extent did you perceive depth?
Q2	How successfully you were able to judge the relative depths of objects in the scene?
Q3	To what extent do you prefer this stereoscopic 3D mode?
Q4	Did you feel any Symptoms from viewing the scenes in stereo (discomfort, blurry vision, eye strain, difficulty concentrating, difficulty focusing, headaches, dizziness, Nausea)?

are designed such that they can be easily used over prescription glasses without any interference to the user.

We chose a within-subjects design for our experiments. Each scene was presented to the participants with both static and dynamic stereo parameters. The users were asked to judge the relative depth of objects in both the scenes (like the cubes in the first scene and other objects in the second scene) and based on that they answered questions about depth discrimination. While performing this judgment task, they did not know if the scene used dynamic stereo or static stereo. In addition, they were asked to rotate their head and not their eyes to look around in both scenes. Each condition was presented to the participants in pre-selected counterbalanced order based on a Latin square design. After the experiment, the participant filled out a post-questionnaire about each scene with questions about depth discrimination, user preference, and visual discomfort (see Table 5.1).

Table 5.2 Results of Wilcoxon signed rank test for qualitative questions. DD: Depth discrimination, JD: Judgment of depth and PF: Preference

Question	Scene 1	Scene 2
DD	$Z = -3.084, p < 0.005$	$Z = -3.078, p < 0.005$
JD	$Z = -3.086, p < 0.005$	$Z = -2.971, p < 0.005$
PF	$Z = -2.810, p < 0.05$	$Z = -2.638, p < 0.05$

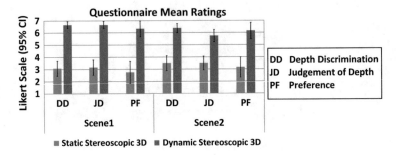

Fig. 5.5 Mean qualitative ratings for both scenes based on type of stereoscopic 3D

5.5   Results

To analyze the Likert scale data, we used Wilcoxon signed rank test with $\alpha = 0.05$. The results for the qualitative questions are summarized in Table 5.2 and mean values are plotted in Fig. 5.5. Compared to static stereo:

- depth discrimination was significantly improved with presence of dynamic stereo.
- significantly more people felt that they were able to correctly judge the relative depths of objects in scenes when dynamic stereo was present.
- significantly more people preferred using dynamic stereo.

Except for one participant, no one felt any significantly negative symptoms by watching the scenes in stereoscopic 3D (static as well as dynamic). One participant was very sensitive to stereoscopic 3D. He experienced moderate eye strain and discomfort with both static as well as dynamic stereo.

5.6   Discussion

Our scenes were designed keeping stereoscopic viewing in mind and used design guidelines from the literature (Kulshreshth et al. 2012; Schild et al. 2013; Schild and Masuch 2011). We chose the separation and the convergence values for each scenario such that the visual discomfort was minimized. During our pilot testing, these values were optimized based on user feedback to ensure that they are comfortable for most users. Most of our user study participants did not experience any visual discomfort with either static or dynamic stereo.

Our study also had some limitations. We used head tracking data to approximate the user's look direction. But, a user may not always be looking straight ahead since the eyes could look in a different direction. We asked our users to rotate their head and not their eyes to look around in the scene. However, this was not natural and could have a minor effect on our results. We expect that using an eye tracker would even further improve our results. We did not consider the variation in interocular distance between the users in our experiments. However, we expect that the results would be similar since our algorithms uses (see implementation details) the ratio of display width (27 inch in our experiment) and interocular distance (between 58 and 70 mm Dodgson (2004)) which is minimally affected by this variation in interocular distance. In addition, our small sample size (12 participants) could have a minor affect on our results.

We would like to mention that the use of dynamic stereo would change the geometry of the scene (e.g. an increase in separation makes the world seem smaller and/or the observer feel larger) and may not be a good idea in situations where scale is of critical importance such as in case of industrial design applications. Regardless, our results indicate that dynamic stereo has potential to improve depth discrimination in stereo 3D applications. Future application designers should use dynamic stereo adjustments to provide a better experience to the user. However, these parameters should be chosen wisely, based on the scene, to minimize visual discomfort.

5.7 Conclusion

We presented two scenarios where optimizing the stereo parameters (separation and convergence) could enhance the depth discrimination of the user. Our preliminary results indicate that participants preferred to use dynamic stereo over static stereo since it significantly improved the depth discrimination in the scene. Our study is a preliminary step towards exploring the effectiveness of dynamic stereo in stereoscopic 3D applications and further research with more scenarios is required.

So far we have seen benefits of stereoscopic 3D and head tracking in games. We also found Finger-Count menus to be the best choice for games. Our next task is to combine all these techniques, based on our results, and design a game which can make best use of all these techniques.

References

Colin W (1995) Dynamic stereo displays. In: Proceedings of the SIGCHI conference on human factors in computing systems. CHI '95. Denver, Colorado, USA: ACM Press/Addison-Wesley publishing co., 1995, pp. 310–316. ISBN: 0-201-84705-1. https://doi.org/10.1145/223904.223944. URL: http://dx.doi.org/10.1145/223904.223944

Dodgson NA (2004) Variation and extrema of human interpupillary distance. https://doi.org/10.
1117/12.529999

Duchowski AT et al. (2014) Reducing visual discomfort of 3D stereoscopic displays with gaze-contingent depth-of-field. In: Proceedings of the ACM symposium on applied perception. SAP
'14. Vancouver, British Columbia, Canada: ACM, 2014, pp. 39–46. ISBN: 978-1-4503-3009-1.
https://doi.org/10.1145/2628257.2628259

Kulshreshth A, Schild J, LaViola Jr JJ (2012) Evaluating user performance in 3D stereo and motion
enabled video games. In: Proceedings of the international conference on the foundations of digital
games. New York: ACM, 2012, pp. 33–40. https://doi.org/10.1145/2282338.2282350

Maiello Guido et al (2014) Simulated disparity and peripheral blur interact during binocular fusion.
J Vis 14(8):13

Margarita V, Allison RS (2014) Gaze-contingent depth of field in realistic scenes: the user experience. In: Proceedings of the symposium on eye tracking research and applications. ETRA '14.
Safety harbor, Florida: ACM, 2014, pp. 119–126. ISBN: 978-1-4503-2751-0. https://doi.org/10.
1145/2578153.2578170

Matthias B et al (2014) The effects of fast disparity adjustment in Gaze controlled stereoscopic
applications. In: Proceedings of the symposium on eye tracking research and applications. ETRA
'14. Safety harbor, Florida: ACM, 2014, pp. 111–118. ISBN: 978-1-4503-2751-0. https://doi.
org/10.1145/2578153.2578169

Michael M et al (2014) Depth perception with gaze-contingent depth of field. In: Proceedings of the
SIGCHI conference on human factors in computing systems. CHI '14. Toronto, Ontario, Canada:
ACM, 2014, pp. 217–226. ISBN: 978-1-4503-2473-1. https://doi.org/10.1145/2556288.2557089

Schild J et al (2013) Creating and analyzing stereoscopic 3D graphical user interfaces in digital
games. In: Proceedings of the SIGCHI conference on human factors in computing systems. CHI
'13. Paris, France: ACM, 2013, pp. 169–178. ISBN: 978-1-4503-1899-0. https://doi.org/10.1145/
2470654.2470678

Schild J, Masuch M (2011) Fundamentals of stereoscopic 3D game design. In: ICEC, International
federation for information processing. 2011, pp. 155–160

Chapter 6
Simultaneous Usage of Several 3DUI Technologies

Abstract In the previous Chaps. 2, 3, 4 and 5, we have studied the benefits of 3DUI technologies (e.g. stereoscopic 3D, head tracking, gesture based control, etc.) for video games. But, the work was focused on these technologies in isolation and was still unknown how the gaming experience will be affected if several 3DUI technologies are used simultaneously. In this chapter, we discuss work related to usage of multiple 3D interaction techniques simultaneously. We also present an experiment which seeks to study the effect of presence of several 3DUI technologies when present in a game simultaneously. Moreover, since no existing game could be used for this experiment, a custom game was designed. The design of this game which optimizes the use of stereoscopic 3D, head tracking, and finger-count based menus is also presented in this chapter.

6.1 Introduction

In the second chapter, we learned that stereoscopic 3D provides user performance benefits in relatively simple scenes where user is interacting with a single object at a time. This approach avoids user distraction and enhances the overall game play experience. Moreover, we also learn that we should avoid too much user motion in front of the display to avoid any sync signal loss issues with active stereoscopic 3D glasses and to reduce geometric errors when leaving the sweet spot for the 3D effect. Head tracking is a good choice for some game tasks since it does not require the users to move too much and users do not have to leave the sweet spot for the 3D effect. In the third chapter, we formally evaluated head tracking and learnt that it could be a good choice for certain games (FPS, air combat). In experiments with stereoscopic 3D (Chap. 2) and head tracking (Chap. 3), the results were dependent on the game play experience of the users. The experienced gamers were able to

© Springer International Publishing AG, part of Springer Nature 2018   83
A. K. Kulshreshth and J. J. LaViola Jr., *Designing Immersive Video Games Using 3DUI Technologies*, Human–Computer Interaction Series,
https://doi.org/10.1007/978-3-319-77953-9_6

make use stereoscopic 3D and head tracking to their advantage. On the contrary, the casual gamers focused more on the basic game mechanics and did not pay much attention to more advanced features like stereoscopic 3D and head tracking. In order to eradicate this problem, we should have some sort of training or in-game hints while playing the game to help casual gamers to make better use of stereoscopic 3D and head tracking. Menu system is also an important part of a game. To avoid breaking the engagement/immersion in game, the gamers need minimal interference from menu systems while playing. We designed faster Finger-Count menus to serve as in-game menus (see Chap. 4). In Chap. 4, we experimentally determined that our Finger-Count menus are fast and efficient and could potentially be used as in-game menus. In the fifth chapter, we learnt that dynamic stereoscopic parameters could enhance depth discrimination in certain scenarios (an application where there is a large variation in depth range across scenes and an application which always has a large object in front of the camera) and is preferred by user's over static stereoscopic 3D parameters.

In the previous Chaps. 2, 3, 4 and 5, we have studied the benefits of 3DUI technologies (e.g. stereoscopic 3D, head tracking, gesture based control, etc.) for video games. But, the past work have been focused on these technologies in isolation and it is still unknown how the gaming experience will be affected if several 3DUI technologies are used simultaneously. By designing a game which integrates several 3DUI technologies, we hope to understand the interplay between the technologies and its effect on the gaming experience. In the next section, we describe an air-combat game which was custom designed which uses design ideas derived from our experiments in previous Chaps. 2, 3, 4 and 5. The main aim of this game is to prove that if the game is designed with 3DUI techniques in mind then these techniques provide better gaming experience to users.

6.2 Related Work

Ware et al. (1993) used a display configuration called Fish Tank Virtual Reality, where there is a desktop system with a stereoscopic display and head-tracking. They conducted two experiments that compared viewing conditions of stereo display versus non-stereo display with head-tracking. In the first experiment, users thought that head-tracking created a more compelling 3D perception than stereo viewing alone. In the second experiment, users performed a tree tracing task. Again, the head-tracking provided the best results. Although head-tracking had better results, the stereo did show significant benefits over normal viewing. Similar results have been found by other research as well. In another study, Arthur et al. (1993), users preferred head tracking, when isolated, over stereo 3D viewing, and while there were benefits shown for stereo 3D in user performance in a tree tracing task, the benefits were greater for head tracking in the same task.

Barfield et al. (1999) studied the effects of stereoscopic 3D and head tracking on a wire-tracing task. Their results indicated that the task time was the same irrespective of display conditions (monoscopic vs stereoscopic 3D) when head tracking was present. People performed best with stereoscopic 3D when head tracking was absent. McMahan et al. (2012) explored the interplay between display fidelity and interaction fidelity. Their results showed that the performance was best with low-display low-interaction fidelity and high-display and high-interaction fidelity. LaViola et al. (2008a, b) explored the effects of head tracking and stereoscopic 3D viewing on the user performance when rotating 3D virtual objects using isomorphic and non-isomorphic rotation techniques. Their results indicate that rotation error is significantly reduced when subjects perform the task using non-isomorphic 3D rotation with head tracking/stereo than with no head tracking/no stereo.

Another experiment involving a spatial judgment task (Ragan et al. 2013) showed that the participants performed better with head-tracking and best performance was achieved when both stereoscopic 3D and head tracking was present. The worst score was achieved with a combination of monoscopic display and no head tracking. However, none of these researchers used complex video games for their experiments. In addition, none of the work mentioned above evaluated the affects of using several 3DUI technologies together in complex gaming environments like in modern video games.

6.3 Design of the Game

We are going to design a game based on the results of our experiments in previous chapters. An air-combat game seems to be a good fit since it requires depth perception to locate enemies around the aircraft and to avoid crashing with other objects (including ground). Furthermore, an air-combat game scene has a lot of depth and using stereoscopic 3D would make the game more immersive. We could take some design ideas from Wings of Prey game (see Chap. 3) since it turned out to be a game which used head tracking efficiently thereby improving users performance when head tracking was present.

Additionally, we wanted to include a 3DUI input mechanism in our game to create a more inclusive 3D user interface experience and chose a gesture-based interface. Initially, we experimented with several motion sensing devices (e.g. Leap Motion, Microsoft Kinect, etc.) but these devices failed for our purposes for two reasons. First, the gestures recognition accuracy of these devices was not good enough for precisely controlling the aircraft in our game. Second, users needed to continuously control the airplane causing fatigue during our pilot testing sessions (lasting for about 100 minutes). These factors hindered the overall gameplay experience. However, finger-count gestures (Kulshreshth and LaViola 2014) are well studied in the past (see Chap. 4) and have higher recognition accuracy as well as being easy to use and fast to perform. These gestures could potentially be used as shortcuts in video games. The finger count gestures were well suited for longer use since the user is not using them continuously while playing the game. Therefore, we used these gestures as an alternate to using buttons for switching weapons. We refer to them as finger-count shortcuts in this chapter.

Most games fix the 3D parameters (convergence and separation) to some optimal values. In real life, our eyes can adjust the convergence distance dynamically and focus on the object of interest. To simulate this reality in games, we would make use of head tracking to find the object of interest, based on where the user is looking, and adjust the convergence distance to the nearest object in that direction. This technique could potentially improve stereoscopic 3D gaming experience and reduce eye strain while playing. Ware (1995) explored adjusting the separation dynamically such that the nearest object is always rendered behind the screen. Their results showed that the separation could be larger than the actual eye separation (approximately 6.3 cm) based on the depth range of the scene and the separation could be changed dynamically without any noticeable scene distortions if the change is made gradually. Our game design also dynamically adjusts stereoscopic 3D parameters (convergence and separation), based on user's look direction, for a comfortable viewing experience and still enhance stereo depth perception whenever possible.

6.3.1 Game Mechanics and Controls

The player has to control an aircraft , using the Logitech extreme 3D Pro joystick, in first person view and shoot enemies (see Fig. 6.1 for a screenshot of the game). The game has five different kind of enemies, each marked with a different color, and five different kind of weapons. The color of the crosshair indicates the color of the currently selected weapon. Each enemy can be killed only with a weapon of the same color and thus requires a user to frequently switch weapons while playing the game. A radar is also available which shows 2D positions of the enemies around the aircraft. To be consistent with the color scheme, the radar uses the same color as the enemy to display its position. The game also featured 3D sound effects for aircraft, weapons and explosions (when enemies are shot dead). An enemy could also be locked (except for yellow and green enemies) by holding the crosshair over it for a short period of time (about two seconds).

The head of the player can be controlled either by using head tracking (a TrackIR 5 device was used) or a combination of the hat switch and buttons on the joystick (see Fig. 6.2). To switch weapons one can use finger-count shortcuts or buttons on the joystick (one button is assigned for each weapon). To avoid any confusion each button is clearly marked with a color on the joystick. In case of finger-count shortcuts, a chart was displayed at the top of the screen indicating the correspondence between finger-count gestures and weapon colors. The game was implemented using the Unity3D game engine and the Air Strike Starter Kit from the Unity Asset Store. For implementing finger-count shortcuts, we used the Intel's perceptual computing SDK.

Fig. 6.1 Air-combat game screenshot

Fig. 6.2 Joystick Controls
for the air-combat game

6.3.2 Stereoscopic 3D Features

Stereoscopic 3D specific GUI elements. Based on Schild et al. (2013), we optimized our game GUI for stereoscopic 3D usage. All the 2D GUI elements (timer, game stats, etc.) were rendered at screen depth to allow them to be in focus throughout the game. The radar was displayed at the bottom of the screen and was also rendered at screen depth. The chart displaying the correspondence between finger-count gestures and weapon colors was a 3D object rendered at the same depth as the aircraft to be visible all the time without being occluded by other 3D objects in the scene.

Optimal depth cues. The game minimized the impact of monocular depth cues. All the enemy ships were colored instead of textured. No dynamic light sources were used and shadows (a known depth cue) were disabled.

Disable post-processing image effects. Some post-processing image effects (e.g. halo effect for lights) do not work well with stereoscopic 3D rendering since these effects are rendered only for one eye making it uncomfortable to look at. Hence, we did not use any post-processing image effects for our game.

Minimized 3D glasses flicker. Excessive motion in front of the display may sometime cause the 3D glasses to flicker due to loss of sync signal (Kulshreshth et al. 2012). In our case head tracking was used only for head rotations and zooming and all other motions were restricted. In case of head rotation, the head position does not change and the head rotation is also limited (about 40 degrees each side). When a user zooms in, the head moves towards the Nvidia IR emitter. Thus, in both these cases the head motion is minimal and does not interfere with 3D sync signal loss. Furthermore, we noticed that Nvidia 3D vision 2 glasses were flickering when used together with the Creative Senzeye3D depth camera (used for detecting finger-count gestures). We suspect that there was some interference between IR blaster inside the camera and the 3D sync signal from Nvidia IR emitter causing the glasses to loose sync signal. However, older Nvidia 3D vision glasses worked fine without any flickering issues. Hence, we used older Nvidia 3D vision glasses instead of newer 3D vision 2 glasses for our experiments.

6.3.3 Dynamic Stereoscopic 3D

Currently, most stereoscopic 3D games fix convergence and separation values for optimal depth budget throughout the game. But, this approach reduces stereo depth when a large object (e.g. a gun in FPS games, the cockpit in air-combat, etc.) is present in front of the game camera. The reason being the fact that stereo parameters have to be optimized to keep that large object always in focus. However, when the player's head is rotated, that nearby object is not in the players view and stereo depth could be increased. In case of our air-combat game, we optimized stereo parameters under two conditions. First, when the user is looking sideways (left/right) and second, when the user is zoomed into the scene. In both these cases, the user is not looking at the cockpit in front. When the player's head is rotated sideways (left/right), the separation is increased with linear scaling proportional to the heads rotation and the convergence is not changed. When a user zooms in the scene the field of view (FOV) of the camera is reduced proportional to the head's displacement. Thus, in case of zooming, the separation is increased with linear scaling proportional to the camera's FOV. At the same time, the convergence is linearly decreased with the camera's FOV to keep both the crosshair and background in focus. These dynamic parameters ensured a comfortable stereoscopic 3D experience and provided better depth perception for this air-combat game.

We used Nvidia's 3D vision for our implementation and thus used the NVAPI library (2018) to change the convergence and the separation. According to the N-VAPI library, the normalized eye separation is defined as the ratio of the interocular (distance between the eyes) and the display screen width. The separation value used in the driver is a percentage of this normalized eye separation and hence is a value between 1 and 100. Convergence is defined as the distance of the plane of intersection of the left and right eye camera frustums. Our dynamic stereo algorithm is described in Algorithm 5.2 in Chap. 5. We set $SF = 3, threshold = 50, C_1 = 30, S_1 = 20$ and $S_2 = 50$ in the implementation. These values were obtained based on several pilot studies.

6.3.4 Head Tracking Features

Natural head movements. People are used to rotating their head for looking around. We mapped head tracking to use these natural movements for looking through the sides of the plane and zooming in. Thus, it is very easy to understand the head tracking usage for our air-combat game.

Adaptable setup. Since every user is different (in terms of height/size and comfortable sitting position), the starting head position in the game was customized for each user. We asked users to sit in their relaxed pose and that was chosen as the starting head position/orientation. The user's motion is then detected relative to that starting pose. Thus, we ensured that each user is comfortable while playing the game.

Training for head usage. A prior experiment on head tracking usage in video games (Kulshreshth and LaViola 2013) found that experienced gamers make better use of head tracking than casual gamers. Casual gamers pay more attention to learning how to play the game and do not use these extra features to their advantage. To avoid this problem, we trained all our participants, irrespective of their gaming experience, to be able to play the game and use head tracking at the same time.

Avoid awkward head movements. We restricted the player's head position/orientation to avoid most awkward head poses. The player's head could only be rotated sideways (left/right) and up/down. The head position was fixed along axes parallel to the display to allow only one directional movement toward display while zooming. These restrictions ensure that the users don't get disoriented while playing thereby reducing head-tracking based motion sickness (nausea).

Non-isomorphic head rotations. When users are looking at the display, they can not rotate their head beyond a certain range depending upon the display size and the player's distance from display. In the past, non-isomorphic rotations seem to have helped in rotation tasks (LaViola et al. 2008b) when head tracking is present. We used non-isomorphic rotation scaling for left and right rotations to allow users to see more area on both sides of the plane without rotating his head too much. We thought this would help them quickly scan a large area of the game environment for finding potential enemies.

6.3.5 Why Five Enemies and Five Weapons?

As part of our experiment, we wanted to evaluate the performance of finger-count
shortcuts, as a fast way to switch weapons, compared to buttons. Since the user were
using one hand to control the plane, only one hand was available for finger-count
gestures. This limits the number of finger-count gestures to five. This motivated us to
keep five different kind of enemies. Moreover, we wanted people to use these gestures
frequently throughout the game play session. Thus, we designed five different kind
of weapons and added a restriction that each enemy can be killed only by a specific
weapon.

6.4 User Evaluations

We conducted an experiment with our air-combat game, see Fig. 6.3, to evaluate the
combined effect of stereoscopic 3D, head tracking, and finger-count shortcuts on the
gaming experience. Additionally, we also looked at the effects of individual technologies to be able to understand their contribution to the overall gaming experience.
Based on previous findings in related work and our analysis of the game, we have
the following hypotheses:

Hypothesis 1 (H1): The combined usage of stereoscopic 3D, head tracking and
finger-count shortcuts improves user's gaming performance compared to the control condition with monoscopic display, no head tracking and buttons for weapon
switching.

Fig. 6.3 A user playing the air-combat game we designed. The game effectively uses stereoscopic
3D, head tracking and finger-count gestures

Fig. 6.4 The experimental setup for the air-combat game user study

Hypothesis 2 (H2): Stereoscopic 3D improves user's gaming performance compared to the monoscopic display condition.

Hypothesis 3 (H3): Head-tracking improves user's gaming performance compared to button based head control.

Hypothesis 4 (H4): User's performance with finger-count shortcuts will be same as with buttons.

Hypothesis 5 (H5): Participants prefer to use Finger-count shortcuts compared to buttons.

6.4.1 Subjects and Apparatus

We recruited 32 participants (29 males and 3 females ranging in age from 18 to 30 with a mean age 20.84) from the university population, of which four were left handed. Out of all participants, only 4 had prior experience with head tracked games, 8 had played stereoscopic 3D games, and 30 people had played motion controlled games. The experiment duration ranged from 100 to 120 minutes and all participants were paid $10 for their time.

The experiment setup, shown in Fig. 6.4, consisted of a 27" BenQ XL2720Z 3D monitor, Nvidia 3D Vision kit, a TrackIR 5 with Pro Clip (mounted on a headphone), a Creative Senz3D depth camera, a Logitech Extreme 3D Pro joystick, and a PC (Core i7 4770 K CPU, GTX 780 graphics card, 8 GB RAM). We used the Unity3D game engine and Intel Perceptual Computing Software Development Kit (PCSDK) for implementing the game. The TrackIR 5 camera, the creative camera, and the Nvidia

IR emitter were mounted on the top of monitor. Participants were seated about 2 feet away from the display. Since the 3D Vision glasses could impact the subjective feel and comfort level of the participants under different condition, participants were asked to wear them throughout the experiment. In non-stereoscopic condition, the open shutters of the glasses provide an image slightly darker than without glasses but minimally brighter than the stereoscopic 3D version. To make sure that all our participants are able to see stereoscopic 3D, we used Nvidia medical test image to test stereo abilities of participants. All our participants passed the test. All participants preferred using their right hand (despite some of them being left handed people) for joystick control and left hand for weapon switching (buttons or finger-count gestures).

6.4.2 Experiment Design and Procedure

We chose a within-subjects design for our experiments in order to be able to measure and compare user perceptions of the game on a variety of quantitative and qualitative metrics. This within-subjects experiment had 3 independent variables: display mode (Stereoscopic 3D and monoscopic 2D), head control mode (head-tracked and button based head control) and weapon switch mode (finger-count shortcuts and buttons). In total we had $2 \times 2 \times 2 = 8$ conditions and for each condition the user conducted two trials which makes a total of 16 game plays per participant as part of this experiment. Each game trial ends if the player dies (if hit with another plane or ground, shot by another plane) or if the time limit of 5 minutes is reached . Our dependent variables were mean survival time and mean number of enemies killed, where the mean is taken over the two trials for that condition.

The experiment began with the participant seated in front of the monitor and the moderator seated to the side. Participants were given a consent form that explained the experiment procedure. They were then given a modified version of Terlecki and Newcombe's video game experience survey (Terlecki and Newcombe 2005) as a pre-questionnaire which collected general information about the participant (age, sex, dexterity) and their prior gaming experience. At the beginning, each participant was trained for about 20-25 minutes on how to play the game under different experimental conditions. Participants then played the game under each condition. Each condition presented to the user in random order based on a Latin square design (Fisher 1935). We recorded survival time, number of enemies killed and head tracking usage data for each gaming condition presented during experiment. After the experiment, the participant filled out a post-questionnaire with questions about their experiences with the game (see Table 6.1) including questions about stereoscopic 3D (see Table 6.2), head tracking (see Table 6.2), and finger-count shortcuts (see Table 6.3).

Table 6.1 Post-questionnaire. Participants responded to question 1–11 on a 7 point Likert scale. Question 12 was a multiple choice question

Game Questions	
Q1	To what extent did the game hold your attention?
Q2	How much effort did you put into playing the game?
Q3	How mentally demanding was this game?
Q4	Did you feel hurried or rushed when playing this game?
Q5	To what extent you felt frustrated while playing?
Q6	To what extent did you find the game challenging?
Q7	To what extent did you enjoy the graphics and the imagery?
Q8	To what extent you felt that you were part of the game rather than just observing?
Q9	To what extent you felt that you were physically present in the game environment presented?
Q10	How much would you say you enjoyed playing the game?
Q11	Would you like to play the game again?
Q12	Which aspects of the game made your overall game experience better? Stereoscopic 3D, Head-tracking, Finger-count shortcuts?

6.5 Results

To analyze the performance data, we used repeated-measures 3-factor ANOVA per dependent variable. We did a post-hoc analysis using pairwise sample t-tests. We used Holm's sequential Bonferroni adjustment to correct for type I errors (Holm 1979) and the Shapiro-Wilk test to make sure the data was parametric. To analyze the Likert scale data, we used Friedman's test and then a post-hoc analysis was done using Wilcoxon signed rank test. For all of our statistical measures, we used $\alpha = 0.05$.

6.5.1 Quantitative Results

Repeated measures 3-factor ANOVA results are shown in Table 6.4. In terms of enemies killed, significant interactions were found based on the combined usage

Table 6.2 Stereoscopic 3D/Head tracking questionnaire. Participants responded to question 1–6 on a 7 point likert scale. Questions 7–10 were multiple choice and open ended questions to gauge the users perception of the effects of stereoscopic 3D. In question 11, each symptom had a 7 point likert scale to indicate the extent of each symptom ranging from not at all to very much so

Stereoscopic 3D/Head tracking questions	
Q1	To what extent did 3D/HT improved the overall experience of the game?
Q2	To what extent 3D/HT was helpful in the game?
Q3	I would choose to play with 3D/HT over normal viewing.
Q4	I felt that 3D/HT enhanced the sense of engagement I felt.
Q5	3D/HT is a necessity for my future game experiences.
Q6	To what extent you felt that the head tracking helped you find enemies in the environment faster?
Q7	Do you feel that 3D/HT helped you to perform better?
Q8	How did 3D/HT help you perform better?
Q9	Do you feel that 3D/HT hurt your performance?
Q10	How did 3D/HT hurt your performance?
Q11	Did you feel any Symptoms from viewing the games in stereoscopic 3D (eye strain, headaches, dizziness, Nausea)?

of all the three technologies (DM×HCM×WSM). People killed significantly more ($t_{31} = -2.546$, $p < 0.02$) enemies when stereoscopic 3D, head tracking and finger-count shortcuts ($\bar{x} = 18.21$, $\sigma = 5.70$) were present compared to a condition with monoscopic display, no head tracking and buttons for weapon switch ($\bar{x} = 15.32$, $\sigma = 4.88$). There was no significant difference in survival time between the above two conditions.

We found significant differences in the number of enemies killed ($F_{1,31} = 14.264$, $p < 0.005$) and the survival time ($F_{1,31} = 14.215$, $p < 0.005$) based on the head control mode (NHT vs HT). Participants killed significantly more enemies ($t_{31} = -3.777$, $p < 0.005$) and survived significantly longer ($t_{35} = -3.770$, $p < 0.005$) when head tracking was present. Mean number of enemies killed and mean survival time under different gaming conditions is shown in Figs. 6.5 and 6.6 respectively. There was no significant difference in the number of enemies killed or the survival time based on the display mode (2D vs 3D). Compared to monoscopic mode, people killed slightly more enemies when stereoscopic 3D was present. We found significant differences in terms of enemies killed based on the weapon switch mode (buttons vs finger-count shortcuts) but no significance was found in the post-hoc analysis.

Table 6.3 Finger-Count Questionnaire. Participants responded to question 1–3 on a 7 point Likert scale. Questions 4 and 5 were yes/no questions. Question 6 was an open ended question

Finger-Count questions	
Q1	To what extent did the finger-count gestures improved the overall experience of the game?
Q2	To what extent did you feel that the finger-count gestures were helpful while game play?
Q3	To what extent do you think that using a finger-count for weapon switch was better than using buttons?
Q4	The finger-count gestures hurt your performance in the tasks that were presented?
Q5	Do you feel that the finger-count gestures should be used for future games?
Q6	Are there any other game tasks (not specific to this game) where finger-count shortcuts could be used?

Table 6.4 Repeated measures 3-factor ANOVA results. DM: Display Mode, HCM: Head Control Mode, WSM: Weapon Switch Mode

Source	Enemies killed	Survival time
DM	$F_{1.31} = 0.876, p = 0.357$	$F_{1.31} = 0.021, p = 0.886$
HCM	$F_{1.31} = 14.264, p < 0.005$	$F_{1.31} = 14.215, p < 0.005$
WSM	$F_{1.31} = 5.320, p < 0.05$	$F_{1.31} = 3.255, p = 0.081$
DM×HCM	$F_{1.31} = 0.103, p = 0.751$	$F_{1.31} = 0.932, p = 0.342$
DM×WSM	$F_{1.31} = 2.601, p = 0.117$	$F_{1.31} = 1.791, p = 0.191$
HCM×WSM	$F_{1.31} = 3.705, p = 0.063$	$F_{1.31} = 0.995, p = 0.326$
DM×HCM×WSM	$F_{1.31} = 6.221, p < 0.05$	$F_{1.31} = 0.009, p = 0.924$

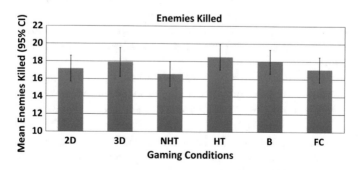

Fig. 6.5 Mean number of enemies killed under different gaming conditions where 2D : Non-stereoscopic 3D, 3D: Stereoscopic 3D, NHT: Non-head-tracked, HT: Head-tracked, B: Button based weapon switch, and FC: Finger-Count based weapon switch

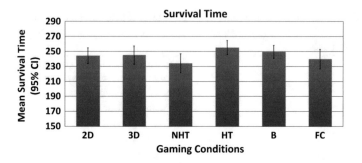

Fig. 6.6 Mean survival time under different gaming conditions where 2D : Non-stereoscopic 3D, 3D: Stereoscopic 3D, NHT: Non-head-tracked, HT: Head-tracked, B: Button based weapon switch, and FC: Finger-Count based weapon switch. Higher survival time is better

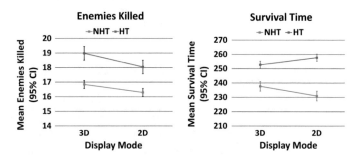

Fig. 6.7 Mean enemies killed and mean survival time irrespective of weapon switch mode where 2D : Monoscopic, 3D: Stereoscopic 3D, NHT: Non-head-tracked mode, and HT: Head-tracked mode

Furthermore, the gaming experience of the participants did not play a significant role in the performance of the participants across different gaming conditions. The statistics were same even when we divided the participants in two groups, casual and experienced, and compared performance data for all gaming conditions separately for two groups.

To compare our results with prior research (Barfield et al. 1999, Ragan et al. 2013), we also looked at the number of enemies killed and the survival times based on only the display mode and the head tracking mode (see Fig. 6.7). We found that people killed most enemies when both head tracking and stereoscopic 3D was present but survival time was slightly more for head tracked (HT) and monoscopic condition. Overall, head tracking played a significant role in performance and stereoscopic 3D had only minor performance impact.

When head control data (see Fig. 6.8) was analyzed, we found that significantly more people, compared to button based head control, used head controls when head tracking was present ($t_{31} = 6.917$, $p < 0.005$). We also found that people use zoom (iron sight) more often compared to looking sideways (left/right).

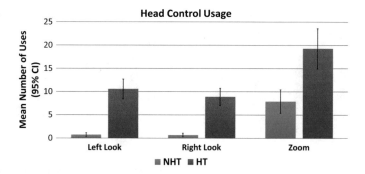

Fig. 6.8 Players head control usage based on head control mode (buttons versus head tracking)

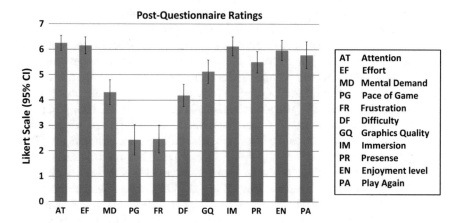

Fig. 6.9 Mean ratings for the game post-questionnaire

Mean ratings for game post-questionnaire questions 1–11 (see Table 6.1) are summarized in Fig. 6.9. We can see that:

- The game held attention of all the participants and everyone tried their best.
- The game had moderate mental demand and difficulty level.
- Participants did not feel frustrated while playing and indicated that they would like to play the same game again.
- Graphics quality of the game was rated as high and people enjoyed the game.

Out of 32 participants, 27 liked head tracking, 22 liked stereoscopic 3D and only 11 liked using finger-count shortcuts (see Fig. 6.10). Majority of participants thought that stereoscopic 3D and head tracking was helpful in the game. Four people thought that stereoscopic 3D hurt their performance and five people thought that head tracking hurt their performance. People were divided about their views on

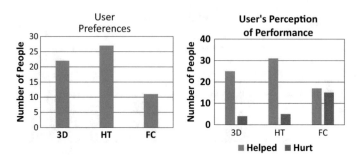

Fig. 6.10 User preferences and user's perception of stereoscopic 3d, head tracking and finger-count shortcutslabelfig

finger-count shortcuts. Out of 32, 17 thought that finger-count shortcuts helped them perform better and 15 thought that it hurt their performance. Nineteen people thought that finger-count gestures should be used for future games.

Users perception of the three technologies revealed some interesting findings. Mean ratings for stereoscopic 3D, head tracking, and finger-count post-questionnaire questions (Q1–Q5 for 3D and HT, Q1–Q3 for FC) are summarized in Fig. 6.11. Overall experience was significantly ($\chi^2 = 11.327$, $p < 0.005$) different across three technologies. Head tracking provided significantly better ($Z = -2.693$, $p < 0.01$) overall experience compared to finger-count shortcuts. Helpfulness of technologies was significantly different ($\chi^2 = 7.856$, $p < 0.05$) across technologies. Head tracking was significantly more ($Z = -2.339$, $p < 0.02$) helpful than finger-count shortcuts. Preference ratings of the technologies were also significantly different ($\chi^2 = 6.018$, $p < 0.05$). Head tracking ($Z = -2.249$, $p < 0.03$) and stereoscopic 3D ($Z = -2.125$, $p < 0.04$) had significantly higher preference rating than finger-count shortcuts. There was no significance found between head tracking and stereoscopic 3D for necessity ratings. People did not think that stereoscopic 3D or head tracking is a necessity for future games. Except for minor eye strain, none of the participants noticed any symptoms (headache, dizziness, or nausea) from viewing games in stereoscopic 3D.

Out of all participants, 17 people thought that the depth perception was better with the presence of stereoscopic 3D, 17 people thought that it was more enjoyable to play with stereoscopic 3D, only 9 people thought that stereoscopic 3D helped them to judge the relative position of the enemies in the game, and 15 people thought that stereoscopic 3D made the game look more realistic. For the head tracking questionnaire, 17 people thought that head tracking added more realism to the game, 26 people thought that it was helping them to find enemies in the game environment, 26 people thought that it was much easier to look around with head tracking, and 25 people thought that zoom feature was helping them shoot distant enemies.

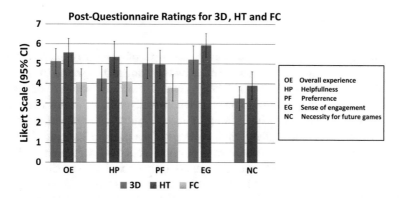

Fig. 6.11 Mean ratings for the stereoscopic 3D, head tracking and finger-count post-questionnaire. Please note that EG and NC ratings were not collected for finger-count shortcuts

6.5.2 Qualitative Results

When asked about their experience playing the game, participants gave a variety of responses. One participant mentioned that he was very impressed with 3D effects in the game and it distracted him while playing. He occasionally felt like just enjoying the view rather than playing the game. Two of our participants were very sensitive to stereoscopic 3D and mentioned that it was very uncomfortable for them to play the game in 3D. One participant mentioned that it was uncomfortable to wear 3D glasses throughout the experiment. Two participants did not like zooming using head tracking because they felt uncomfortable being close to display screen while playing. Few participants mentioned that it was much easier to use finger-count shortcuts than buttons because they don't have to look down to find the button corresponding to a enemy color.

We got some interesting ideas when they were asked for other possible game tasks where finger-count gestures could be useful. One participant suggested to use finger-count gestures to quickly select and send pre-assigned text messages to other gamers in a multiplayer gaming environment. Currently, this task requires using a mouse which may not be the fastest choice. Another participant mentioned that finger-count gestures could be useful to solve some mini-puzzles, requiring selection from a set of items (e.g. Tower of Hanoi puzzle in Mass Effect where the task is to move blocks between towers), in games. A few other comments include using finger-count gestures to switch between different characters in a multi-character game (e.g. Trine), to switch between items in the minecraft game, to teleport a game character to different numbered locations in the game, and to assign a task (from a set of numbered tasks) to a game character.

6.6   Discussion

We found significant performance benefits, in terms of number of enemies killed, due to combined usage of stereoscopic 3D , head tracking and finger-count shortcuts. Survival time was similar compared to the condition with monoscopic display, no head tracking, and button based weapon switch. Essentially, it means that people killed more enemies in the same time as in the condition with none of these technologies present. Therefore, the combined usage of the three technologies improved the performance of the users and we were able to accept out first hypothesis H1.

We did not find any significant performance differences based on display mode. These results are not surprising because prior experiments which studied effects of stereoscopic 3D (Litwiller and LaViola 2011, Schild et al. 2012, 2014) also found similar results. Kulshreshth et al. (2012) found performance benefits of stereoscopic 3D for some video games (a pool table game and a game involving manipulation of 3D blocks) depending upon the user's prior gaming experience. But, those games were very different from our air-combat games and had tasks requiring precise motion in three dimensional space. For our game, the aircraft was moving in 3D space and enemies could be locked which does not require that much precision to shoot. Hence, we were not able to accept our second hypothesis H2.

Our experiment indicates that participants performed significantly better, in terms of enemies killed and survival time, when head tracking was present. Availability of head tracking helped participants find enemies faster in the environment without rotating the whole aircraft. When they were using button based head controls, it was not as easy to control the head as in case of head tracking which used natural head movements for controlling the player's head. Occasionally, while turning, participants used head tracking to make sure the turn is safe and would not end up in a collision with mountains or the enemies in the vicinity. Based on these results, we accepted our third hypothesis H3.

Most participants were positive about the game and felt an enhanced sense of engagement while playing when stereoscopic 3D and/or head tracking was present. They mentioned that depth perception, due to presence of stereoscopic 3D, made the game very realistic and more enjoyable. They felt as if they were actually flying that plane. Furthermore, they mentioned that it was very natural to use head tracking for searching enemies and it made the game very realistic. It was also mentioned that the gaming experience was best when both head tracking and stereoscopic 3D was present.

User's performance with finger-count shortcuts was as fast as with buttons and we were able to accept our fourth hypothesis H4. We expected these results based on the fact that the recognition time for our finger-count gestures (under a second) was approximately same as that of a button press. Moreover, it has already been shown that finger-count gestures are easy to learn and fast to perform (Kulshreshth and LaViola 2014). Consequently, all participants were able to learn these gestures quickly and use them for weapon switching task in the game.

Interestingly, people were divided about their views on finger-count shortcuts. About half of participants preferred using finger-count shortcuts while another half did not. One possible reason could be familiarity with the button based interfaces (game controllers, keyboard/mouse, etc.) for video games. Most people play games using button based game controllers. Some of them like motion controlled games and some don't. Another possibility could be higher cognitive demand associated with finger-count shortcuts. In case of finger-count shortcuts, they need to control both hands independently and in different spatial areas requiring more cognitive attention than pressing buttons on a joystick. Consequently, we were unable to accept our fifth hypothesis H5.

Gaming experience of participants did not play a significant role in performance across different gaming conditions. In prior experiments with stereoscopic 3D (Kulshreshth et al. 2012) and head tracking (Kulshreshth and LaViola 2013), it was found that gaming performance across different gaming conditions could be affected by gaming experience of the participants. Casual users focus more on playing the game rather than using added features (head tracking or stereoscopic 3D) to their advantage. Meanwhile, expert users try to use these additional features to improve their game play performance. Our air-combat game was an easy game to play and all participant were allowed to practice the game, for about 20–25 min, before the experiment began. This gave them ample time to get themselves familiar with the game and not worry about learning the game during the actual experiment. This could have been the reason we did not noticed any significant interactions based on the participants prior gaming experience.

Compared to prior research (Barfield et al. 1999, Ragan et al. 2013), which studied interaction between head tracking and stereoscopic 3D, our results (see Fig. 6.7) were slightly different. In our case, we found that head tracking significantly improved performance but stereoscopic 3D did not. Barfield et al. (1999) found that display mode did not affect performance when head tracking was present and performance was better with stereoscopic 3D when head tracking was absent. Ragan et al. (2013) found that performance was best when stereoscopic 3D and head tracking was used together, but provided little benefit when used individually. One possible explanation of this difference could be the difference in the tasks presented to the participants as part of the experiment. Barfield et al. (1999) used a wire tracing task, in which the objective was to move a virtual stylus (controlled by a real stylus) along the path of a virtual wire as quickly as possible without touching the wire. In case of Ragan et al. (2013), participants inspected cave structures with layers connected by vertical tubes and the task was to count the number of tubes connecting the horizontal layers. In both experiments, these were simple isolated tasks which were very different from playing a video game requiring a user to pay attention to many things while game play.

We found that people used head controls more often when head tracking was present. In case of button based head control, a combination of joystick hat switch and buttons (see Fig. 6.2) was used to control the head of the player. On the other hand, when head tracking was present, natural head head movements were used to perform the same task. Cognitively, using buttons was much more difficult than using head tracking. Hence, while game play people refrained from using head controls frequently when head tracking was absent.

There are a few factors that could have affected our results. Our implementation of stereoscopic 3D, using dynamic stereo parameters, was different from all the past implementations. This could have a minor effect on our results but we still believe that the results will be similar or worse (due to less depth perception) with fixed stereo parameters. The size of display screen used could also have some influence on how much users can turn while using head tracking. The ideal choice would be very wide and curved display, with 180 degree field of view, but such stereoscopic 3D displays are not easily available. Most participants in our user study were males and this gender imbalance could have a minor effect on our results.

6.7 Conclusion

We presented an in-depth study which investigates how the combined use of several 3D user interface technologies affects the gaming experience. We designed an air-combat game keeping stereoscopic 3D, head tracking, and finger-count shortcuts usage in mind based on existing design ideas from the literature. A within subjects experiment was conducted where we examined game performance data, head tracking usage data, and data on user perception of the game. Our results show that people perform significantly better with the combined use of these technologies. Additionally, we found that head tracking was a major contributor to these performance benefits. The finger-count shortcuts also did not add much to the performance. However, about half of our participant preferred to use finger-count shortcuts compared to buttons for switching between weapons.

In this chapter, we have shown that simultaneously using several 3DUI technologies could provide a better gaming experience if the game is designed with the usage of these technologies in mind. In the next chapter, we discuss our experiments from previous chapters and propose some directions for future work.

References

Arthur KW, Booth KS, Ware C (1993) Evaluating 3D task performance for fish tank virtual worlds. ACM Trans Inf Syst 11(3):239–265

Barfield W, Hendrix C, Bystrom K-E (1999) Effects of stereopsis and head tracking on performance using desktop virtual environment displays. Presence: Teleoper Virtual Environ 8(2):237–240. https://doi.org/10.1162/105474699566198 ISSN: 1054-7460

Fisher RA (1935) The design of experiments. Oliver and Boyd, England

Holm S (1979) A simple sequentially rejective multiple test procedure. Scandinavian J Stat 6(2):65–70

Kulshreshth A, LaViola Jr JJ (2013) Evaluating performance benefits of head tracking in modern video games. In: Proceedings of the 1st symposium on spatial user interaction. SUI '13. ACM, USA, pp 55–60. https://doi.org/10.1145/2491367.2491376

Kulshreshth A, LaViola Jr JJ (2014) Exploring the usefulness of finger-based 3D gesture menu selection. In: Proceedings of the SIGCHI conference on human factors in computing systems. CHI '14. ACM, Canada, pp 1093–1102. https://doi.org/10.1145/2556288.2557122 ISBN: 978-1-4503-2473-1

Kulshreshth A, Schild J, LaViola Jr JJ (2012) Evaluating user performance in 3D stereo and motion enabled video games. In: Proceedings of the international conference on the foundations of digital games. ACM, NY, pp 33–40. https://doi.org/10.1145/2282338.2282350

LaViola JJ et al (2008a) Poster: effects of head tracking and stereo on non-isomorphic 3D rotation. In: IEEE symposium on 3D user interfaces, 2008. 3DUI 2008, pp 155–156. https://doi.org/10.1109/3DUI.2008.4476614

LaViola JJ et al (2008b) The influence of head tracking and stereo on user performance with non-isomorphic 3D rotation. In: Proceedings of the 14th eurographics conference on virtual environments. EGVE'08. Eurographics Association, Eindhoven, pp 111–118. https://doi.org/10.2312/EGVE/EGVE08/111-118 ISBN: 978-3-905674-06-4

Litwiller T, LaViola Jr JJ (2011) Evaluating the benefits of 3D stereo in modern video games. In: Proceedings of the SIGCHI conference on human factors in computing systems. CHI'11. ACM, USA, pp 2345–2354. https://doi.org/10.1145/1978942.1979286

McMahan RP et al (2012) Evaluating display fidelity and interaction fidelity in a virtual reality game. IEEE Trans Vis Comput Graph 18(4):626–633. https://doi.org/10.1109/TVCG.2012.43 ISSN: 1077-2626

Nvidia's NVAPI Library (2018) https://developer.nvidia.com/nvapi.

Ragan ED et al (2013) Studying the effects of stereo, head tracking, and field of regard on a small-scale spatial judgment task. IEEE Trans Vis Comput Graph 19(5):886–896. https://doi.org/10.1109/TVCG.2012.163 ISSN:1077-2626

Schild J et al (2013) Creating and analyzing stereoscopic 3D graphical user interfaces in digital games. In: Proceedings of the SIGCHI conference on human factors in computing systems. CHI '13. ACM, France, pp 169–178. https://doi.org/10.1145/2470654.2470678 ISBN: 978-1-4503-1899-0

Schild J, LaViola Jr JJ, Masuch M (2012) Understanding user experience in stereoscopic 3D games. In: Proceedings of the SIGCHI conference on human factors in computing systems. CHI '12. ACM, USA, pp 89–98. https://doi.org/10.1145/2207676.2207690

Schild J, LaViola Jr JJ, Masuch M (2014) Altering gameplay behavior using stereoscopic 3D vision-based video game design. In: Proceedings of the SIGCHI conference on human factors in computing systems. CHI '14. ACM, Canada, pp 207–216. https://doi.org/10.1145/2556288.2557283 ISBN: 978-1-4503-2473-1

Terlecki MS, Newcombe NS (2005) How important is the digital divide? the relation of computer and videogame usage gender differences in mental rotation ability. Sex Roles 53:433–441

Ware C (1995) Dynamic stereo displays. In: Proceedings of the SIGCHI conference on human factors in computing systems. CHI '95. ACM Press/Addison-Wesley Publishing Co, USA, pp 310–316. https://doi.org/10.1145/223904.223944 ISBN: 0-201-84705-1

Ware C, Arthur K, Booth KS (1993) Fish tank virtual reality. In: Proceedings of the INTERACT '93 and CHI '93 conference on human factors in computing systems. CHI '93. ACM, Amsterdam, pp 37–42. https://doi.org/10.1145/169059.169066 ISBN: 0-89791-575-5

Chapter 7
Discussion and Future Work

Abstract This chapter discusses the implications of the experiments discussed in previous Chaps. 2–6 and preposes some directions for future research.

7.1 Discussion

In this book, we explored several 3D user interface technologies to make a better gaming experience. The work was focused on improving game play experience by using stereoscopic 3D, head tracking, and faster gesture controlled menus. We first studied each of these technologies in isolation to understand their benefits for games. Based on the results of these isolated experiments, we custom designed an air-combat game to use all the three technologies simultaneously and studied how it affects the gaming experience. Our experiments indicate that 3D user interface technologies could make gaming experience better if used effectively. However, the games must be designed to make use of the 3D user interface technologies available in order to provide a better gaming experience to the user.

Not all games could be optimized for a given 3D user interface technology. Our studies with stereoscopic 3D and head tracking indicated that game genre (which relates to types of interactions in the game) is an important factor in the choice of 3D user interface technology. We saw that participants performed better with stereoscopic 3D only in games (Hustle Kings and Tumble) which have 3D tasks where the user is manipulating a single object at a time and the scene is more or less static. A game with only 2D tasks will never benefit from the presence of stereoscopic 3D. In addition, the 3D tasks should require depth perception to be able to perform better with stereoscopic 3D. However, other depth cues (such as shadows) could also be used to judge depth. Therefore, we can minimize/disable using other depth cues in case stereoscopic 3D is present. Other 3D user interface technologies, when present simultaneously, could also affect the role played by stereoscopic 3D. In our last experiment (see Chap. 6), we found that head tracking was a dominant factor in user performance. Although users performed slightly better with stereoscopic 3D, the presence of head tracking helped them perform significantly better (see Fig. 6.7). Our head tracking experiment (see Chap. 3) indicates that users perform better in

© Springer International Publishing AG, part of Springer Nature 2018
A. K. Kulshreshth and J. J. LaViola Jr., *Designing Immersive Video Games Using 3DUI Technologies*, Human–Computer Interaction Series,
https://doi.org/10.1007/978-3-319-77953-9_7

case of a first person shooter game and an air combat game. Both these game genres use natural head gestures for controlling the game camera. Fast paced games, such as racing games, are not a good candidate for head tracked games.

Gaming expertise of a user could significantly affect user performance when 3D user interface technologies are present. For games which are too easy to play (such as Microsoft Flight), the presence of 3D user interface technologies may not provide any additional benefits to expert gamers. Expert gamers play games very often and can perform equally well without the presence of 3D user interface technology (such as head tracking) if the game is too easy to play. However, casual gamers may learn faster in such easy games when a 3D user interface technology is present. In case of moderately complex games (such as Arma II), experts have an edge over casuals. Expert user can learn to play the game faster and can make better use of additional 3D user interface technology to their advantage. Meanwhile, casual gamers appear to focus more on games basics and do not pay much attention to the 3D user interface technology present. In case of our stereoscopic 3D experiment (see Chap. 2), we saw that expert users can also make use of other depth cues (such as shadows) and may not learn faster, compared to monoscopic condition, when stereoscopic 3D is present. Therefore, to alleviate the affect of gaming expertise on performance in our last experiment (see Chap. 6), we asked participants to play the game for a while before the actual experiment began. As indicated by our results, this training phase helped participants not only to learn the game but also to use the presence of 3D user interface technologies to perform better. Thus, it is very important to teach the usage of 3D user interface technologies to gamers before they could make use of these technologies to their advantage. A training level at the beginning of a game may be very helpful to achieve this.

A menu system can significantly affect user experience in games. We explored the utility of finger count gestures for selection tasks in games. We found that finger-count gestures (or shortcuts) have high selection accuracy since are easy to understand and fast to perform. However, people were divided about their views on finger-count shortcuts usage in our last experiment. Overall, we found that performance with finger-count shortcuts was as fast as with buttons. Surprisingly, about half of participants preferred using finger-count shortcuts while another half did not. Most people play games using button based game controllers and such familiarity could be the reason for this. Some of them like motion controlled games and some don't.

As part of our experiments, we studied three 3D user interface technologies: stereoscopic 3D, head tracking, and gesture controlled menus, and their interactions when all these technologies are present simultaneously. Our results show that people perform significantly better with the combined use of these technologies if the game is designed with the usage of these technologies in mind. Therefore, it is very important to integrate game tasks, during the design phase, which could benefit from the 3D user interface technologies present.

7.2 Future Work

There are many 3D user interface technologies available in the market. We explored some of them as part of this work. However, we believe that there are many opportunities for this research to be continued and extended. This section offers suggestions on how to build upon this work further over the next few years.

7.2.1 More Game Genres

In our experiments with stereoscopic 3D and head tracking, we used a few game genres to study the benefits of these technologies. Our experiments are a preliminary step towards exploring the effectiveness of stereoscopic 3D and head tracking in realistic game scenarios. Clearly, further research with more game genres is required to further validate our results.

In our final experiment with all the technologies present simultaneously, we studied only a single game genre (an air-combat game). In the future, it would be interesting to explore these technologies for other game genres as well. For example, a game genre that could benefit from all these technologies is first-person-shooter games. Stereoscopic 3D would be helpful to judge the depth of distant enemies, head tracking would be helpful to quickly find enemies in the environment, and finger count gestures could be used for either switching weapons or teleporting the game character to other predesignated areas of the game environment.

7.2.2 Multi-session Experiments

All our experiments were conducted in a single session per participant. We did not study how the gaming experience is effected with varying duration of the experimental time. Playing the game for different durations (e.g., 20 min, 40 min, or 60 min every other day for two weeks) might affect the game experience and would be interesting to look at in the future. The challenging part here would be to find participants who can commit for such long duration multi-session experiments.

7.2.3 Better Demographics

The sample population we used for our experiments were mostly university students between the ages of 18 to 30. In addition, most participants were males. These factors could have an effect on our results. In the future, more experiments with a wider range of age groups with balanced gender could be performed to further validate our results.

7.2.4   Dynamic Stereo Algorithm Improvements

The dynamic stereo algorithm we developed in Chap. 5 (see Algorithms 1 and 2) is a very preliminary algorithm and relies on head tracking data to approximate user's look direction. But, a user may not always be looking straight ahead since the eyes could look in a different direction. We asked our users to rotate their head and not their eyes to look around in the scene. However, this was not natural and could have a minor effect on our results. We expect that using an eye tracker would even further improve our results.

In our dynamic stereo experiment, the values of the stereo parameters were determined based on our pilot studies. However, we believe that these values could be expressed in terms of display size, distance of the user from the display, and distance of the object being looked at in the scene. One could explore this direction in future work. Furthermore, we did not consider any quantitative measures as part of this work. Future research could include depth judgments tasks (e.g. Howard-Dolman test 1919) in the experiments to quantify the differences between dynamic and static stereo scenes.

Furthermore, the algorithm developed uses optimizations specific to the air-combat game we designed. A generic algorithm which optimizes stereoscopic 3D parameters (convergence and separation) would be more desirable. Such an algorithm could be used for any game scene and it optimizes the parameters based on the depth information obtained from the scene. Best case scenario would be an implementation at graphics driver level. However, the graphics driver source code is not accessible to general public. We used Nvidia's NVAPI (Nvidia 2018) library to interface with the graphics driver and modify stereo parameters on the fly while game play. Stereoscopic 3D game designers should consider using this library during the game design phase and use some dynamic stereo optimization to enhance the game play experience.

7.2.5   Educating Stereoscopic 3D Gaming

Naturally we see stereoscopic 3D due to presence of two eyes in our body. Each eye sees a different view of the world in front of us and thus creates the disparity needed to generate a stereoscopic 3D image perceived by our brain. We are trying to simulate that in a stereoscopic 3D display system. However, stereoscopic 3D is an unnatural binocular effect since the objects are rendered on a flat/2D surface of the display. Thus, it requires a user to cope up with this effect to perceive depth and make better use of it in their game play. Games could be designed to educate the users to make use of stereoscopic 3D in a step by step process. This could include instructions on how to properly setup the stereoscopic 3D system based on the user's preference, what game tasks could benefit with presence of stereoscopic 3D, and some tutorial level which teaches how to make use of stereoscopic 3D to perform better.

Furthermore, not all users can use same stereoscopic parameters (convergence and separation). Depth tolerance level of each user is different depending upon how much much stereoscopic 3D content they use. Casual gamers can not always tolerate the same depth effect as the expert gamers. Therefore, it is very important for a game to include a parameter setup step at the beginning along with instruction on how to change the stereo parameters with shortcut keys while game play.

7.2.6 Display Technology

Currently, we need 3D glasses to watch stereoscopic 3D content on a stereoscopic 3D display. This requirement limits the frequent use of stereoscopic 3D content (e.g. video games) mainly because of three reasons. First, 3D shutter glasses reduce perceived brightness of the display due to shuttering of the glasses. Second, the glasses are uncomfortable for long duration usage. And last, some users don't like to use glasses. Dodgson (2005) proposed that the future will be all about autostereoscopic displays. Many major display manufacturer (e.g. Toshiba, Samsung, Vizio etc.) are working on autostereoscopic display technology. These displays have the potential to change the user experience significantly. When such displays become available, more experiments will be needed to explore how this technology affects the user's gaming experience. Recently in 2014, many manufacturers have released curved displays with 4K resolution which may provide more immersive user experience. In future, such display could also be explored to see if they provide a better gaming experience.

7.2.7 Virtual Reality Games

Virtual reality gaming is where a person can experience being in a three-dimensional environment and interact with that environment during a game. In the past, virtual reality games/application were mostly limited to commercial applications and research labs. A new commercial approach for gaming in virtual reality (VR) was started with the Oculus Rift virtual reality headset. In comparison to earlier attempts, the device offers a wide field of view and low latency to head posture updates at a low mass-market compatible price point, which gained a lot of positive reactions. Since then many VR headsets have been made available to consumers including HTC Vive, PlayStation VR, Samsung Gear and Google Daydream VR. These VR devices offer more immersion and a totally different gaming experience compared to a traditional desktop based setup. However, using stereoscopic 3D and head tracking on this device might provide an entirely different user experience. Further exploration with many game genres could explore how this device compares to a traditional stereoscopic 3D display (e.g. Monitor, TV, etc.) in terms of gaming experience. In addition, we need to explore more 3D interaction techniques which could provide an interface which is more natural and easier to use in the VR environment.

References

Howard HJ (1919) A test for the judgment of distance. In: Transactions of the American Ophthalmological Society, vol 17. pp 195–235
Nvidia's NVAPI Library (2018) https://developer.nvidia.com/nvapi
Dodgson NA (2005) Autostereoscopic 3D Displays. In: Computer, vol 38.8. pp 31–36 ISSN: 0018-9162. http://doi.ieeecomputersociety.org/10.1109/MC.2005.252

Chapter 8
Summary and Conclusion

Abstract This chapter summarizes our research experiments, discussed in prior chapters, on utilizing 3D interaction technologies for improving the gaming experience. In the end, we conclude the book.

Modern games use several 3D user interface technologies to enhance game play. Several 3D interaction devices and displays are available to the consumer but their use in games is still not optimal. We need better guidelines for game developers to make use of these technologies in an efficient manner. Stereoscopic 3D have been explored in the past but it was found useful only for certain isolated tasks. An understanding of factors that affect stereoscopic 3D gameplay experience is very crucial to game designers to be able to use it effectively. Head tracking has been explored for virtual/augmented reality tasks but it has not been explored much for its usefulness in modern games. Research must be performed to study how head tracking could be used effectively in modern video games. We also need fast and effective menu techniques to make game play experience better. Another interesting question is how the gaming experience is effected when several 3D user interface technologies are present in the game simultaneously. In the next section, we summarize our experiments conducted towards finding answers to the questions discussed above.

8.1 Summary of Our Experiments

In this book, we studied three 3D user interface technologies: stereoscopic 3D, head tracking and finger-count gestures. First, we studied each of these technologies in isolation to understand how they affect gaming experience and if we could benefit from its usage. Based on the results of the isolated experiments, we custom designed an air-combat game to use all the three technologies simultaneously and studied how it affects the gaming experience.

The first user study explored the benefits of stereoscopic 3D in modern motion controlled games (Kulshreshth et al. 2012). The results reveal that performance in 3D interaction gaming does not automatically benefit from 3D stereoscopic vision.

© Springer International Publishing AG, part of Springer Nature 2018   111
A. K. Kulshreshth and J. J. LaViola Jr., *Designing Immersive Video Games Using 3DUI Technologies*, Human–Computer Interaction Series,
https://doi.org/10.1007/978-3-319-77953-9_8

Interestingly, 3D stereo can specifically provide a significant performance advantage over 2D vision in rather isolated tasks, when users are manipulating one object at a time and when a scene is more or less static. In simple scenes impact of 3D stereo on performance is much greater than in complex games where many dynamic factors (camera perspective, enemy behavior, and other animated elements) around the interacting object influence the course of the game. A third important finding is that game expertise has the potential to nullify this effect, as observed in the Tumble game. A possible reason is that gamers may have learned to rely on other cues than binocular disparity (e.g., on shadows and lighting). Hence, beginners are more open to using new visual cues and thus benefit more from using 3D stereoscopic vision. Additionally, our qualitative data indicates that 3D stereo is perceived to be more enjoyable and immersive than 2D viewing only for the games which provide an advantage in 3D stereo. This outcome contradicts previous findings, which reported preference for 3D stereo although no advantages in performance were found (Litwiller and LaViola 2011; Rajae-Joordens 2008). These results lead to our conclusion that games need to be particularly designed to allow a benefit in performance from stereoscopic vision.

In the second user study, we explored the benefits of head tracking in modern video games (Kulshreshth and LaViola 2013). We observed that head tracking could provide significant performance advantages for certain games depending upon game genres and gaming expertise. Our results indicate that head tracking is useful in shooting games (FPS, air combat etc.) and it is not a good idea to use it in a fast paced racing games. However, not all users benefit equally well with head tracking. We found that head tracking provided significant performance advantages only for expert gamers. One possible reason could be the fact that head tracking was an added feature in all the games we tested. So it was up to the user whether to take advantage of head tracking or not. While expert gamers could make better use of head tracking, casual gamers appeared to focus more on games basics and did not pay much attention to head tracking. Training users to play the game before the actual experiment might help casual users to take advantage of head tracking and perform better.

In the third study, we explored usefulness of Finger-count based menus and compared it with Hand-n-Hold, Thumbs-Up, and 3D Marking menus using different layouts and modes (novice and expert) (Kulshreshth and LaViola 2014). Our results show that Finger-Count menus are a viable option for 3D menu selection tasks with fast response times and high accuracy and could be well suited for gesture controlled applications such as games. We found that selection time and selection accuracy of Finger-Count menus does not change with layout. We found that Finger-Count menus are fast and are preferred by majority of participants. These menus could be very useful for some in game tasks (e.g. may be used as shortcuts).

In our fourth user study, we explored how can we optimize stereoscopic 3D using dynamic stereoscopic 3D parameters. We presented two scenarios where optimizing the stereo parameters (separation and convergence) could enhance the depth discrimination of the user. Our preliminary results indicate that participants preferred to use dynamic stereo over static stereo since it significantly improved the depth discrimination in the scene. Future application designers should use dynamic stereo adjustments to provide a better experience to the user. However, these parameters should be chosen wisely, based on the scene, to minimize visual discomfort.

Based on the results of the above experiments, we custom designed an air-combat game which integrates all three technologies (Stereoscopic 3D, head tracking, and finger-count shortcuts) and studied the combined effect of these technologies on the gaming experience. Our game design was based on existing design principles for optimizing the usage of these technologies in isolation. Additionally, to enhance depth perception and minimize visual discomfort, the game dynamically optimizes stereoscopic 3D parameters (convergence and separation) based on the user's look direction. We conducted a within subjects experiment where we examined performance data and self-reported data on users perception of the game. Our results (Kulshreshth and LaViola 2015) indicate that participants performed significantly better when all the 3DUI technologies (stereoscopic 3D, head-tracking and finger-count gestures) were available simultaneously with head tracking as a dominant factor. We explored the individual contribution of each of these technologies to the overall gaming experience and discussed the reasons behind our findings.

8.2 Conclusion

3D user interface technologies could make gaming experience better if used effectively. The games must be designed to make use of the 3D user interface technologies available in order to provide a better gaming experience to the user. We explored some technologies (stereoscopic 3D, head tracking, and finger-count gestures) as part of this work and obtained some design guidelines for future game designers. As the technology advances, new 3D user interface technologies will keep coming in the market and further exploration on how they affect the gaming experience will be required. We hope that our work will serve as the framework for the future explorations of making games better with usage of 3D user interface technologies.

References

Kulshreshth A, LaViola JJ Jr (2013) Evaluating performance benefits of head tracking in modern video games. In: Proceedings of the 1st Symposium on Spatial User Interaction. SUI '13. ACM, New York, NY, USA, pp 55–60. https://doi.org/10.1145/2491367.2491376

Kulshreshth A, LaViola JJ Jr (2014) Exploring the usefulness of finger-based 3D gesture menu selection. In: Proceedings of the SIGCHI Conference on Human Factors in Computing Systems. CHI '14. ACM, Toronto, Ontario, Canada, pp 1093–1102. https://doi.org/10.1145/2556288.2557122 ISBN: 978-1-4503-2473-1

Kulshreshth A, LaViola JJ Jr (2015) Exploring 3D user interface technologies for improving the gaming experience. In: Proceedings of the SIGCHI Conference on Human Factors in Computing Systems. CHI '15. ACM, Toronto, Ontario, Canada, pp 124–134 ISBN: 978-1-4503-2473-1

Kulshreshth A, Schild J, LaViola JJ Jr (2012) Evaluating user performance in 3D stereo and motion enabled video games. In: Proceedings of the International Conference on the Foundations of Digital Games. ACM, New York, NY, pp 33–40. https://doi.org/10.1145/2282338.2282350

Litwiller T, LaViola JJ Jr (2011) Evaluating the benefits of 3D stereo in modern video games. In: Proceedings of the SIGCHI Conference on Human Factors in Computing Systems. CHI'11. ACM, New York, NY, USA, pp 2345–2354. https://doi.org/10.1145/1978942.1979286

Rajae-Joordens RJE (2008) Measuring experiences in gaming and TV applications. Probing Experience, vol 8. Philips Research. Springer, Netherlands, pp 77–90 ISBN: 978-1-4020-6593-4

Printed in the United States
By Bookmasters